e ing

in everyday life

gareth knight

© Gareth Knight, 2001, 2013

Published in Great Britain in 2013 by Skylight Press, 210 Brooklyn Road, Cheltenham, Glos GL51 8EA

First published in volume form in 2001 by Sun Chalice Books, Oceanside, USA. Individual essays originally appeared in the following journals: *Quadriga, Light, Open Centres*, and the book *Psychology and the Spiritual Traditions* edited by R.J. Stewart.

All rights reserved. Except for the quotation of short passages for the purposes of criticism and review, no part of this publication may be reproduced, stored in a retrieval system or transmitted, in any form or by any means, electronic, mechanical, photocopying, recording or otherwise, without the prior consent of the copyright holder and publisher.

Gareth Knight has asserted his right to be identified as the author of this work.

Designed and typeset by Rebsie Fairholm
Publisher: Daniel Staniforth
Cover photograph by Rebsie Fairholm

www.skylightpress.co.uk

Printed and bound in Great Britain by Lightning Source, Milton Keynes. Typeset in Monarcha 10.5pt. Titles set in Maestrale, a font by Catharsis Fonts.

British Library Cataloguing in Publication Data.
A catalogue record for this book is available from the British Library.

ISBN 978-1-908011-34-3

contents

1. Esoteric Training in Everyday Life 5
2. The Meditation Process 13
3. The Tree of Life as Image of God 19
4. The Tree of Life as Model of the Universe 34
5. Reflections on Life and Spirituality 51
   Celebration of the Forces of Life 51
   Patterns of Community 52
   The Shadow Side of Spirituality 53
   A Knight of the Drawn Sword 55
   The Other Side of the Door 56
   Bearing the Burden of the Shadow 58
   The Spiritual Director 59
   Preparation for the Great Transition 61
   Poetry and the Spiritual Dimension 64
6. The Importance of Coleridge 69
7. The Impact of Psychology on Esoteric Societies 91

esoteric training in everyday life

ESOTERIC teachings cover such a vast panorama that there seems a danger that they can become an end in themselves. The aspirant is so busy assimilating yet more vistas of possible realisation that he gives no thought to how they might be applied. Thus it may seem that the esoteric student has a built-in tendency to be ineffectual. This, however, is not entirely the case, for the training for adepthood is complex and long, and an attempt to practise before one is qualified can be as foolhardy as say a medical student attempting a little private surgery in his second year. A simple diagram may help to explain the mechanics of training that are involved.

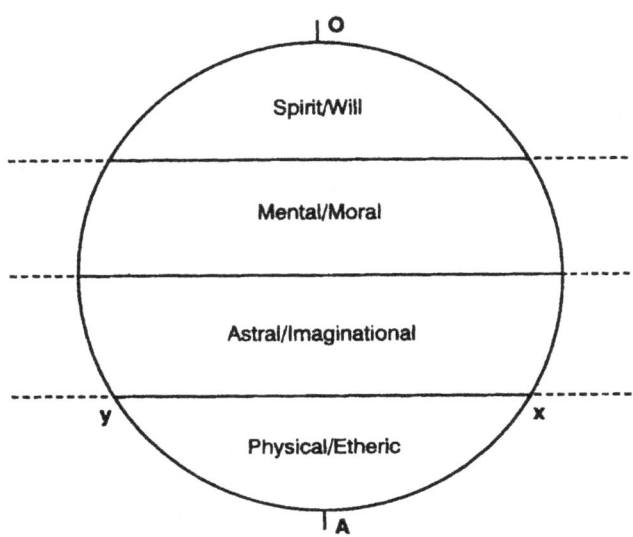

Figure 1: The Cycle of Involution and Evolution

A student who is equipped to commence esoteric training might be regarded as being at point **A**. That is, reasonably well established in the physical world and functioning at least moderately efficiently as a member of prevailing society. If the intending student has major problems integrating with contemporary life than he may be regarded as not having properly reached point **A**. If point **x** represents physical birth, point **y** physical death, then point **A** is a mature person, at terms with the world.

If he or she is somewhere between **x** and **A** then there is a lack of maturity. This may be due to physical age, which is the reason why some esoteric groups do not accept students before the age of 25 or 30. Their argument is that until at least that age the incarnating spirit should be applying itself to establishing itself in physical earth conditions, rather than diverting its energies prematurely to problems of the inner worlds. There will be a temptation for one who commences esoteric training too early to short circuit back up the planes, by a regression to infantilism (perhaps manifesting as over-reliance on the group or some other mother substitute) rather than crossing the nadir of accepting the responsibilities of individual adult life in the physical world.

Physical age is not the only factor, however, for people mature earlier or later in life, and in some respects few of us are ever fully mature; we have hang-ups of one kind or another that cause us to act in childish ways on occasion. But while full and perfect maturity may be too strict a criterion to expect, the custodians of esoteric training need to head off those who fly to the occult as a possible means of escape from the problems of life. As Dion Fortune once said, if one cannot handle the problems of one plane how can one possibly expect to handle the problems of another plane as well? Occultism is no soft option.

Those at point **A** who take up esoteric training are, in point of fact, receiving tuition in matters that normally the soul comes to only after physical death. Hence initiation has been called a living death. This may sound very dramatic but it is technically an accurate description.

Initiation is also, in the broader sense, a speeding up of the natural evolution of the soul's journey. All will reach the goal of human destiny in the end, (save, perhaps, a deliberately perverse few). The initiate simply gets there a little quicker, and is expected to pay for his assisted passage in terms of service to the great majority.

The first true contact of the soul with the Mysteries whilst in the physical world is, in its way, an initiation, and an important one. It is sometimes called the Initiation of the Nadir and marks the point when the spirit manifesting in its physical vehicle can receive an impress direct across the planes from God. On the diagram it is a contact between point **A** and point **O**. In *The Cosmic Doctrine* this is called the Initiation of the Logos, "which marks the transition from the involutionary to the evolutionary arc, for it wakens the Divine Spark which has well and truly been called the 'God within' and which evolves into union with the 'God without'."

Psychic development that may occur before this awakening to objectivity of the Divine Spark can only be retrogressive. It is to be met with in various books of the "self-help" variety that purport to teach ways of influencing people or events. Whatever the effectiveness of their methods in the short term, their personal, divisive and materialistic bias contradicts fundamentally the principles of the higher realities of the inner worlds. Ineffectively applied, they are an attempt to escape from everyday problems in a delusive manner. Successfully applied (which is rare, but possible) they are an entanglement with black magic and entities that seek to drag the soul back to a more primitive state against the tide of natural personal evolution. This is, technically speaking, a degradation rather than an initiation.

Having passed the Nadir and taken up Mystery training, the initiate looks to the opening of consciousness to the higher spheres, which may be through the application of various techniques – prayer, meditation, asanas, mantra, ritual – according to the methods favoured by the particular school to which allegiance has been given.

All properly contacted schools aim at the development of the powers of the soul by service to a hierarchy of achieved adepts or masters (who may or may not be considered to be physically incarnate themselves) by what is perhaps best described as an apprenticeship system. The neophyte, of any grade, learns by helping in the particular tasks of his immediate superiors.

In the earlier stages of the Path, the initiate may well have little conscious understanding of the wider implications of what he is doing, just as the apprentice technician in a great research laboratory might have little realisation of the purpose of the test tubes he washes or the reagents that, under supervision, he prepares. All he is called upon to do is to give of his best until, by virtue of teaching and experience, he is found worthy of greater tasks. Then his, or her, understanding of the overall situation may well increase, but only at the expense of a corresponding increase in responsibility to be carried.

There is, therefore, no easy answer to the question of how one should apply magic or esoteric training to the outer world. One finds a teacher one feels one can trust and allows oneself to be led.

It is no empty symbolism that the candidate for initiation is depicted as blindfolded and stumbling. The first tests of the Mysteries are discretion and discrimination, and this applies very much to the seeking and finding of a genuine teacher appropriate to one's own type and condition of soul. Once the true individual way is found though, it leads forward to greater and greater realisation over a period of years. Instant enlightenment may be possible for the rare soul in rare conditions – usually the God-intoxicated mystic with a particular high destiny – but it is not the normal way of the servers of the Masters of the Wisdom. Their Mysteries may be an accelerated evolution of consciousness but they are not an immediate transformation of it. Still less are they available in six easy lessons; they demand a lifetime's commitment.

The task of the neophyte is to render himself sensitive to the impressions available to him from his inner teacher. These may be in the form of actual teachings to be disseminated to others, or of actions to perform in the outer world, or perhaps, and even more difficult, a change of attitude or personal realisation which in itself will have an effect upon the general social, emotional, mental and moral climate of the times, either in the narrower or the wider sense.

In the narrower sense it may affect a particular group – professional, social or whatever – of which the aspirant is a member. In the wider sense it could affect the nation, race, or even humanity at large.

The effective outer plane teacher is one, therefore, who leads his pupils to make their own contacts. The less effective teachers tend to block off their pupils' expanding realisation by standing in the way of the light, thus casting their own shadow, rather than illumination, upon their students. This can, at its worst, be deliberate or unconscious power seeking, or simply a confusion of function, leading to what might be called an attempt at initiation by photocopier.

Such a group forms simply to receive teachings via one or two sensitives within the group. This may be well enough if the teachings so imparted lead to the recipients developing their own contacts, but there is sometimes the all too human tendency for independent contacts to be discouraged, with the consequence that the more promising students may have to leave in order to develop.

This they may well do successfully but it is not necessarily in their own best interests, as they lose the power and potential guidance a good group should give; and it is not in the best interests of the group, which loses the seed corn of the next generation. Thus such groups tend to wither away but throw up new groups from former members.

However, many esoteric students, perhaps the majority, work on their own. It is not essential to esoteric development to be a paid up member of an occult fraternity. It is true that membership of a group, or personal tuition by an individual, can be a great help, but developing inner awareness is essentially a lone and personal business, and guided by books, journals and the occasional open conference or convention, it is possible for the individual to win through to accepted discipleship of an inner plane order.

If the desire is formulated and held, it sets up a vibration upon the astral plane that will attract the attention of the inner teachers and the way will be opened. It may be opened in a way hardly expected, but open it will, and the way to the summit then consists simply of taking the next step and the next and the next, utilising all the current opportunities and circumstances no matter how unpromising they may appear. The lone worker may follow some false trails, or stand wasting time outside illusory doors that membership of a group or personal study under a teacher might have avoided, but on the other side of the coin it is equally possible to be led astray by fellow students or to be inadvertently misguided by a teacher, all of whom are subject to human error. However, the persistently held desire and dedication is the Ariadne's thread that will lead to the goal by whatever route through the labyrinth.

The inner teachers as we are best able to contact them are all imagination. As one of them stated through Dion Fortune's contact: "What we are you cannot realise and it is a waste of time to try to do so, but you can imagine us on the astral plane and we can contact you through your imagination, and although your mental picture is not real or actual, the results of it are real and actual."

It is for this reason that accepted disciples are somewhat reluctant to reveal the supposed identity of their contacts, except to trusted colleagues. The mode of contact, if of an imagined figure of a famous person from history, is likely to excite only ridicule from the outer world, or delusions of grandeur from the aspiring neophyte.

Let us take as a hypothetical example a figure such as King Henry V, which might well provide a symbolic focus for a higher entity to transmit teachings and powers related to the national interest of England. The hero of Agincourt, the reformed wildling prince, rendered into great literature by Shakespeare, could be a potent focus for inner realities needful to the nation today. We may not necessarily be in touch with the soul or spirit of the discarnate historical personage, whose real life circumstances might have been far from our idealised picture, but it can be important to believe that we are, at the time of the contact. It is another facet of Coleridge's "willing suspension of disbelief" that we practise at any film or theatrical performance or in reading a novel.

Thus, following on from the statement we quoted above, we get the amplification: "...the Masters as they are supposed to be in popular would-be esoteric thought are pure fiction; but as long as you are a 'concrete' consciousness you will have to use the astral to reach the abstract. It is the laws of the astral thought form that are taught in occult science."

If we refer again to our first diagram it will be seen that the astral plane is but a transitory state prior to raising consciousness to higher realities. Thus our contacts with the inner plane teachers should lead us in due time to a direct mind to mind contact; to what might be called mediatorship as opposed to mediumship.

Mediumship, although useful in its place and properly controlled, is in fact an astralism that, by the negative nature of its technique (as in hypnosis, the subject being almost completely passive), tends to regress up the involutionary path rather than to lead forth upon the evolutionary way. The direct mind to mind contact is an entering into a positive fellowship with higher beings which, in due time, passes naturally into a higher still at-one-ment with spiritual actualities.

Thus, to resume the Master's comments: "The difference between the man who touches astral imagination only, and the man who by astral imagination touches spiritual actualities, is that the former in his concepts can rise no higher than the astral imagination and the latter has in his soul spiritual realisation and aspiration which he brings through into 'brain consciousness' by means of the astral imagination."

Thus the outer teachings of occultism are a technology of the imagination. By applying the pictorial faculty to particular symbolic images that inspire and expand the mind, the student is led on to a general opening up of the higher powers of consciousness – ultimately to the union of the 'God within' and the 'God without' after which one needs no other teacher.

Imagination is one of the great pillars of the portal of initiation. The other dynamic pillar is motive, or spiritual intention. If this is weak then we have the soul who has to be content with returning to the general drift of human evolution, for the Mysteries will be too demanding. If, however, the active will be powerful, but perverted

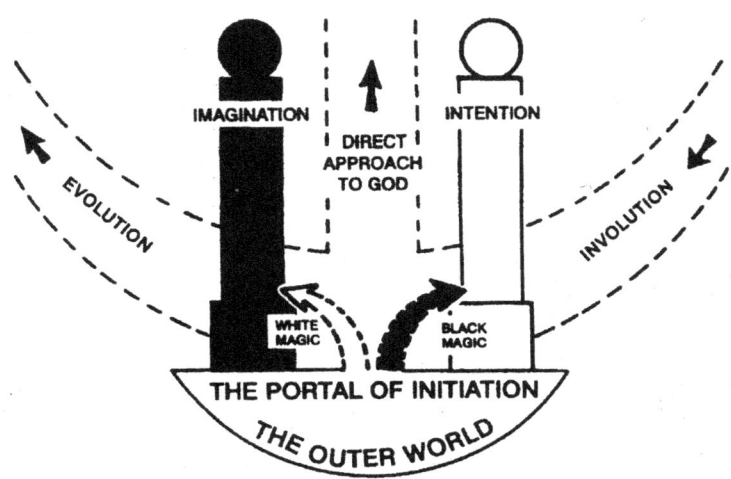

Figure 2: The Portal of Initiation

to personal gratification and power, then by tracking back up the involutionary way it will become a tool of atavistic or evil forces. This is the great divide between white magic and black.

Figure 2 summarises the situation. It will be seen that there is another, direct approach to God. This similarly starts beyond the pillars of Will and Imagination but is a straight and demanding way for the very few to tread. It is also, however, a communication line, as it is the vehicle of the Initiation of the Nadir, which was rendered open to the world at large and not just to initiates, in approximately 30 AD. The significance of this cosmic event may give food for thought in considering the above, and Qabalists may also find some amusement and instruction in applying the two diagrams to the Tree of Life or to Dion Fortune's *The Cosmic Doctrine*.

Originally published in Quadriga 14: Summer 1980

the meditation process

It is best to regard meditation as a process – as a means to some end – rather than as an end in itself. This is because there are so many meanings put upon the word.

For instance, there is a great divide between what might be called occult meditation and the mystical meditation that forms a part of Christian religious experience. Yet sometimes there is no very clear cut distinction made between them, particularly as one type of meditation can lead into another.

As a case in point, the Spiritual Exercises of Ignatius of Loyola commence as occult meditation, albeit on religious subject matter (the visualisation of dramatic scenes in the imagination) but only as a prologue to the purely mystical meditation that is a colloquy of the soul with God. This latter end tends to be overlooked by occult practitioners who like to cite St. Ignatius as a kind of proto-occultist.

By concentrating upon the end in view we are less likely to confuse ourselves. It is also very appropriate, in that a key question to all who seek entry to the Mysteries is "What seek ye?"

This is not so easy to answer as we might at first think. Are we who seek to meditate looking for a process that takes us towards God, or towards ourselves, or away from ourselves, or away from the world, or to a greater awareness of the world, or towards knowledge, or power, or health, or freedom? To suit these various ends, various methods of meditation are likely to be appropriate.

Again, much depends on how we define God, how we define our selves, and how we define the world, if such things are indeed definable.

It may help if we take certain categories one by one and see where they lead us. Using terms in the broadest sense we might divide the whole subject into three areas:

>that of mystical meditation,
>that of occult meditation,
>and that of the meditation of perception.

Mystical meditation has as its object direct conscious communion with God. It is therefore very close to prayer, though not necessarily the formal prayer of petition that characterises much public worship. In mystical meditation the whole focus of consciousness is centred upon God and the whole desire is for communion with God, and for nothing else besides.

This also means that there must first be faith in the existence of a personal God who is willing to respond. We can hardly commune with someone we do not believe in. Nor can we have a very fruitful relationship with a kind of abstract cosmic substance that some Buddhist and esoteric schools seem to see as the ultimate reality. Bliss there may be in a state of nirvana but the question remains: is it communion with God or with an inner ground of consciousness of our own self? This is too complex an issue for us to pursue here but has been analysed in Professor R.C.Zaehner's *Mysticism – Sacred and Profane*.

There are two main types of mystical meditation – the positive way and the negative way.

The positive way uses images, and is the natural human way of thinking – using visualised images of things or people to act as symbolic or prismatic foci of a higher reality. This is the *via positiva* and probably its most sustained and all-embracing example is to be found in that apotheosis of High Medieval mystical theology *The Divine Comedy* of Dante.

The negative way is somewhat more rigorous in that it firmly eschews any image of God, on the grounds that God is unknowable in terms of images of nature or human conceptualisations. Thus direct contact is sought without recourse to pictorial images. The great classic of the *via negativa* is *The Cloud of Unknowing* by an anonymous medieval English mystic. It approaches God by the simple use of one word, chosen almost at random.

A similar method and intention are found in the Jesus Prayer of the Greek Orthodox church, or indeed in such devotions as the Rosary in Roman Catholicism, wherein short prayers are repeated over and over, though associated with the latter are the "positive" imagery of Jesus and the Virgin.

Although the mechanism is superficially similar this is not the same as mantra yoga, which is more properly a form of occult meditation wherein a kind of hypnoidal trance is fostered in conjunction with deep regular breathing exercises. Although occasionally used, breath control techniques are specifically advised against in Orthodox mystical circles. This is perhaps because things can go badly wrong if the intention and techniques are not correct. There are cases of members of small religious sects working themselves into a dangerous form of hysteria through repeating the name "Jesus" or some similar formula ceaselessly hour after hour. They have found themselves not with God but under a psychiatrist.

Let us now consider **Occult Meditation**. Its main function would perhaps be better expressed if we called it soul meditation, for it is a process of opening up higher reaches of self-awareness.

This may be figuratively, in a "downwards" direction, into what we choose to call the subconscious; or "upwards" into what some would call the superconscious. Although these are convenient labels to use, their facility should not blind us to the fact that we know little about either state, except that each seems "bigger" than personal everyday consciousness.

This whole area is the province of depth psychology as well as of yoga and its equivalents. Yoga means "union" and is a conscious interconnection of parts of the psyche and physical vehicle that in the ordinary run of things are separate or connected unconsciously.

Thus yoga in most of its forms is a means of dominating vehicles of the self – be it the mind, the emotions, or the physical functions – sometimes in a spectacular and even bizarre way. But although the ability to suspend the heart beat, to generate great heat, or even to project the etheric double may be formidable achievements, they are a branch of physical and mental callisthenics rather than of religion. One does not have to be a yogi to find God; nor do those who know God necessarily acquire unusual powers over their psycho-physical functions.

Most western forms of soul meditation do not, of course, develop the full yoga curriculum. This really demands conditions of withdrawal from ordinary life that are not easily found in the west. The ancient western meditation tradition, perhaps best epitomised in the works of Plotinus, is one that does not concentrate on physical postures or breathing techniques, except in an ancillary way. It seeks a stilling of the mind and emotions so that the still small voice of the spirit may be heard and eventually take a greater part in the conduct and consciousness of daily life.

Plotinus called this the union of the Lower with the Higher Self; and using various terminologies, many schools of occultism and psychotherapy follow similar objectives and methods. The process is usually depicted symbolically by visualising the integration of two triangles, a downward pointing one representing the Higher Self and an upward pointing one representing the Lower Self. Their conjunction forms the six-pointed Star of David, sometimes elaborated into the Seal of Solomon.

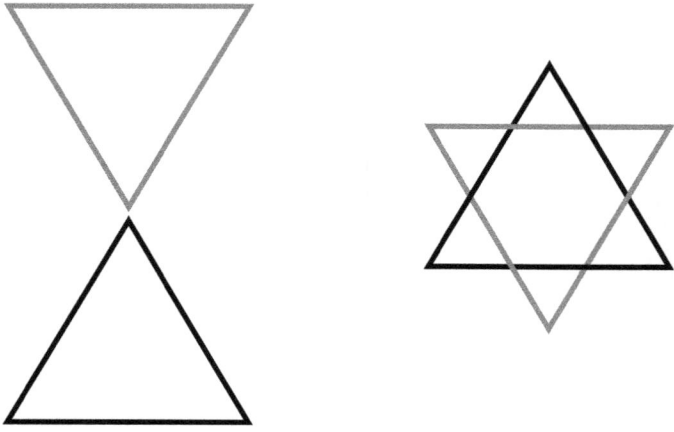

Figure 3: Union of the Higher and Lower Self

Unless we are of the persuasion that the innermost spirit of man is of the same substance as God, and a part of God, there is plainly a great divide between mystical meditation – seeking God – and occult meditation – seeking the Higher Self. The case can be cogently argued either way in theological terms.

This is an important and fundamental issue but one that tends to be either fudged or ignored by many modern occult authorities. It is one that can, all too easily, be ignored; for if the one God is regarded as no more than a vast but vague expansiveness, then even relatively minor expansions of consciousness may give the impression that we are expanding into God consciousness.

Yet this is not necessarily so. God awareness may well come as an indirect result of occult meditation exercises, and a great and joyful surprise it is likely to be, but it is an altogether different experience from the expansion of our own intuitive or higher imaginative faculties.

The **Meditation of Perception** also covers a broad field and one which, by lack of definition, is prone to confusion. The most common and superficial form is embodied in the oft repeated maxim that many people feel closer to God in the fields than in church.

This may be true, so far as it goes, but it tends to confuse God the Creator with certain parts of the creation. Nature as "the luminous garment of the Creator" can be a helpful conception; but we should not confuse the hat with the head that wears it. It is an attitude parallel to the church-goer who feels closer to God by talking to the vicar. In a sense there is a truth in both attitudes, but in an indirect and diluted fashion.

Those with second sight or trained psychism may indeed be aware of great presences in nature at large. These are not necessarily to be worshipped as God any more than we would worship a pet dog. They are simply beings of nature, and even though they may, like an elephant, be bigger than man, they are not necessarily superior except in certain limited areas of strength. In short, we may well have fairies at the bottom of our garden, but this does not mean that they will guide us either to God or to self-realisation.

It is of course possible to utilise the images of nature as pointers to God or to the hidden parts of the self. In this sense nature acts as a mirror (Blake's "vegetable glass") to either God awareness or self awareness by meditating upon it. This has been expressed perhaps in its highest form by the romantic poets, particularly by Wordsworth in, for example, *The Prelude*.

We have analysed the meditation process in a threefold manner, leading to:

    a) a greater awareness of God;
    b) a greater awareness of Self;
    c) a greater awareness of Nature.

Their common denominator is an expansion of awareness; a greater ability to "see", which Teilhard de Chardin considers an important function of the process of survival and planetary evolution.

Thus meditation can only do good. But there is some confusion in defining exactly what that good is. For some the new "seeing" will be towards God, for others towards the Self, for others towards Nature.

In the Mysteries, whether of religion, the self, or nature, right motive is all important. And meditation is thus rather like the Holy Grail that contains the innermost mystery. It demands that we put certain pertinent questions before the enchantment can be lifted from the Godless, self-blind man with the clouded doors of perception.

From Quadriga 11: Autumn 1979. Originally published in "Light".

3

the tree of life as image of god

THE TREE of Life (Figure 4) is the ground plan upon which a great deal of occult knowledge is based. Knowledge not only of the world about us but of the inner worlds. The world that we see with our physical senses is simply an outer shell of a very complex series of inner dynamics, and occultists have made a point of making a study of these psychic forms and forces.

However, when the Tree of Life of the Qabalah was first conceived it had little to do with many of these ideas. There are different approaches to the Tree but broadly speaking we find that most Qabalistic textbooks say that up in Kether is God, and down in Malkuth is the physical world, and all between are the inner worlds between God and the earth.

Well that is fair enough. That is a way of looking at it, and a valid way of looking at it. But it was not the way the Jews conceived it. It was not the way either, that as late as the 17th century, occultists such as Robert Fludd conceived it. In fact the modern conception is a relatively recent one.

It is worth considering a remark of Professor Gershom Scholem, who is perhaps the world's leading authority on Jewish mysticism and the Qabalah, who in the first chapter of *Major Trends in Jewish Mysticism* dismisses modern occult exegesis of the Tree of Life as "highly coloured nonsense" having nothing to do with real Jewish mysticism or the Qabalah.

There is obviously a communication gap here and the least we can do is to see what the basis is for Professor Scholem's remarks. Let us examine what it was that the original Jewish Qabalists started off with, because we can fall into some very serious errors if we do not keep this in mind.

As far as the Jewish Qabalah is concerned the Tree of Life is an image of God.

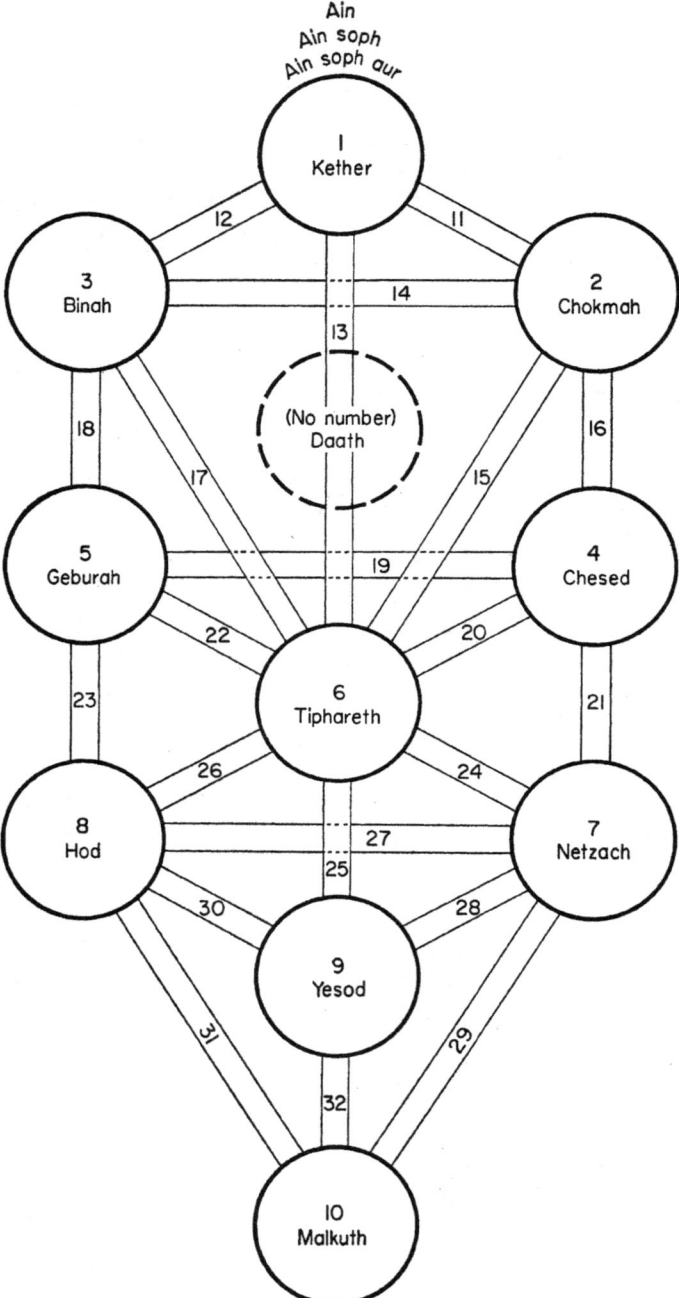

Figure 4: The Tree of Life

Modern occult textbooks on the Tree of Life teach that behind Kether, which is the highest spiritual point that one can conceive, are the Three Veils of what is called Negative Existence. From this state appears the first emanation of creation, coming out of nothingness in three stages, *Ain, Ain Soph, Ain Soph Aur*, which mean Nothingness, the Limitless, and Limitless Light. This agrees broadly with the original Jewish conception but it has been rather unfortunately influenced by 18th and 19th century rationalism. To the Jewish mystics who formulated the Qabalah it is not so much Nothingness in an abstract philosophical sense. To them, before the worlds were created, before there was any creation at all, there was God. All and everywhere.

So when God decided to create worlds and creatures and so on, what could He do? He Himself filled up everything, so first He had to create a vacuum. This is the Qabalistic doctrine known as the *tsim-tsum*, which means making a void within Himself.

There are various ways in which we could visualise this. We could imagine God creating the worlds within the void of His cupped hands; or perhaps making a crystal ball which becomes the sphere within which all the worlds, space and time, form. In the traditional Tree of Life symbolism the void he makes is symbolised by the Three Veils – Nothingness, the Limitless and Limitless Light. The Three Veils should thus go all the way round the Tree of Life.

God then makes Himself present within this Void and manifests Himself in ten different ways. These ten different ways are described in the attributions of the Spheres of the Tree of Life as the God Names and titles, that signify the Crown of Creation, Wisdom, Understanding, Mercy, Justice, Beauty, Victory, Splendour, the Foundation, and last of all, in Malkuth, the Shekinah.

The modern Qabalist talks of Malkuth, the lowest Sephirah, as the physical world, but it is not so to the Jewish Qabalist. To the Jewish Qabalist it is the Shekinah, or Presence of God, and if you read the Old Testament you will see references to this. It is the presence of God over the tribes of Israel which guides them and appears to them as smoke or vapour coming out of the tabernacle, or as a pillar of cloud by day and pillar of fire by night which guides them. Malkuth is the Presence of God to his chosen people.

It also follows that if the Tree of Life represents God, all the Sephiroth or spheres are equal, and this perhaps is better seen in alternative diagrammatic representation. We are all used to seeing the Tree of Life spread out in triadic form but there are other ways of looking at it.

There is one representation of the Tree of Life where the first manifestation of God within the Void is in the centre with the subsequent emanations around this (Figure 5). So we have Kether in the middle, expanding and revealing itself in succession as Wisdom, Understanding, Love, Justice, Beauty and so on until eventually God is fully expanded and fully taken up in His potential as a creating rather than as a completely indrawn Godhead.

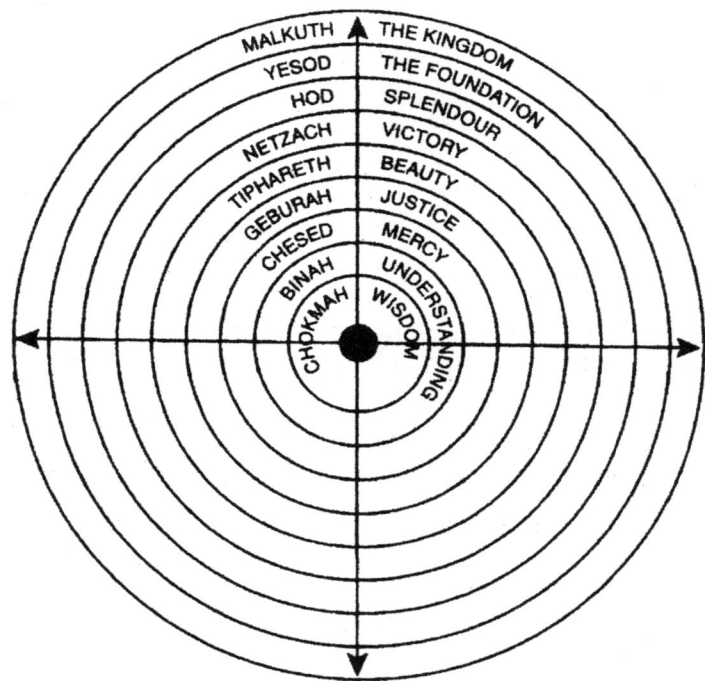

Figure 5: Concentric Tree – the Crown contained in the Kingdom

An alternative perspective is the converse of this as shown in Figure 6. This depicts God creating the Void within Himself and then gradually expanding His influence inwards so we end up with Malkuth in the centre. This emphasises that, as part of His creation, we are completely surrounded by the Shekinah, or Presence of God, then God as Foundation, Splendour, Victory, Beauty and so on.

THE TREE OF LIFE AS IMAGE OF GOD

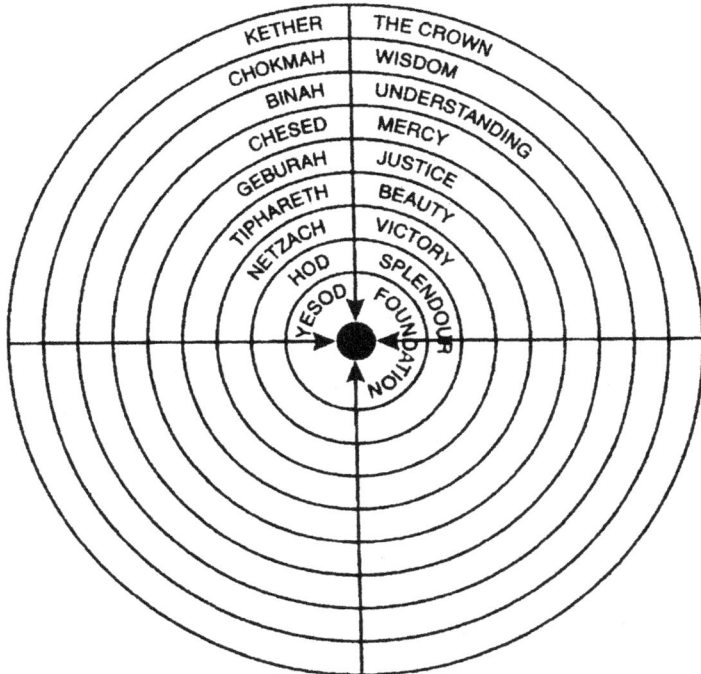

Figure 6: Concentric Tree – the Kingdom contained in the Crown

Figure 7 shows another way, with God showing Himself in balanced Beauty and with various developments of this all around Him as the spokes of a wheel. This again shows that we are not talking about an abstraction gradually getting more concrete, which has led a lot of modern occult Qabalists to assume that matter is a long way from God and that the nearer to matter you get the more prone to evil you become. That is a long way from the original conception.

I think if we want to get some idea of the original conception as it appeared to the Jewish Qabalists then we have to go to the Old Testament, which is the devout Jew's supreme guide. When Moses went up on Mount Zion he saw the Vision of God Face to Face and came down with the Tablets of the Law.

The Tablets of the Law in the first instance were not the Ten Commandments. When Moses came down from the mountain he saw his people reverting to their old Egyptian worship of the golden calf. In horror he dropped the tablets and they broke. The

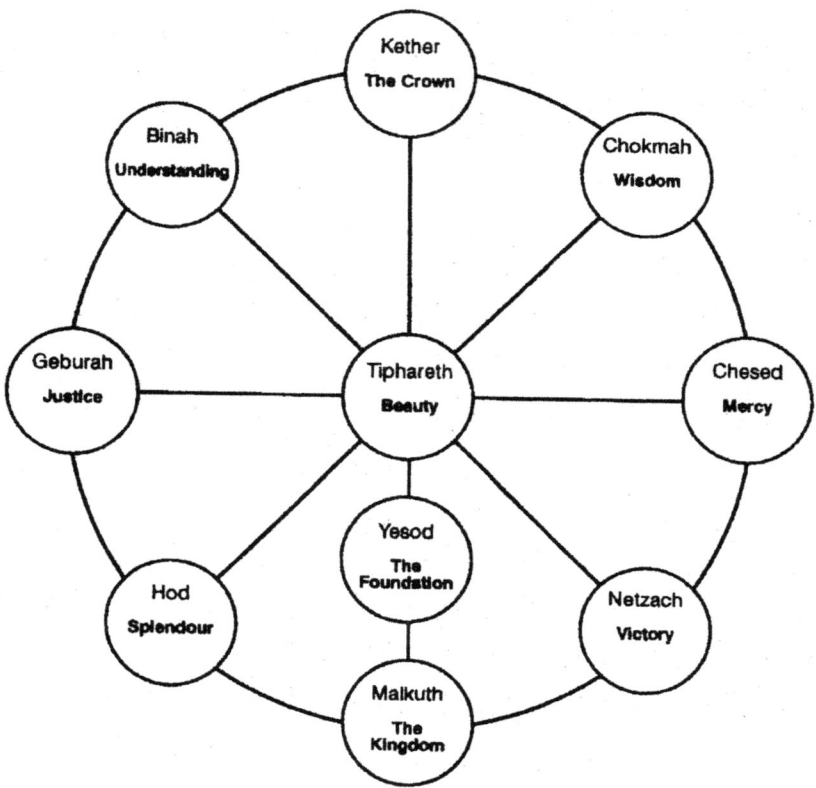

Figure 7: The Tree of Life as a wheel

Ten Commandments, the "Thou Shalt Nots," represent a system of morality which replaced the original law of creation. It is a system made necessary by the Fall or Primal Sin of man, which the Jews were acting out again in spite of themselves.

The original vision of Moses and the Law was not a list of "Thou Shalt Nots." It was summed up by Jesus later as a two-fold love: love of God and love of fellow men.

This conception of God's law for His creation can be conceived as the sum total of the first three Sephiroth, of the Crown, Wisdom and Understanding.

It is also relevant to some early esoteric Jewish texts related to what is called the Throne or Chariot mysticism. (A throne in this context may be conceived as a chariot without wheels; or a chariot as a throne with wheels.) The Vision of Ezekiel for instance, in the

Old Testament, is very much a Qabalistic text. If we read through it we recognise the symbolism of pillars, revolving wheels, a starry canopy, a sea of coals. The starry canopy is similar to Chokmah and the sea of coals underneath is akin to Ashim, the Souls of Fire. And there is a great figure riding in this mighty symbolic chariot.

This was one view of direct communication with God by the Jewish mystics, and in Jewish mystical texts of this type we find accounts of a holy man entering the chariot and going up to God as, for instance, did Elijah. This is not naïve pictorial superstition, it is very high mystical symbolism. This attitude towards God pertains to this day in Islam, where they tend to have a very remote conception of God, or Allah, who is like an oriental potentate on his throne. That is throne or chariot mysticism. A conception of a high God and akin to the three first Sephiroth.

A later conception, in about the first to third century AD, is a Jewish document called the *Sepher Yetzirah*, or Book of Formation. This, as it were, moves us down in our approach to God from the throne or chariot mysticism of a High Being barely comprehensible to man, to trying to understand God by basic archetypal principles of number. In the Hebrew language number and letter are the same, are interchangeable. The *Sepher Yetzirah* is a very small book and is perhaps the first Qabalistic text, using the word Qabalah in the narrow sense, for there is a great deal of Qabalistic material in the Old Testament.

It describes the Cube of Space (see Figure 8) which is simply a cube on which are the 22 letter/numbers of the Hebrew alphabet, split up into three main divisions. First are the three "mother" letters, which are outside the system.

These are:

ש **Shin**, which is the fire of the spirit, placed above the Cube;

מ **Mem**, which represents the waters of creation placed below the Cube;

א **Aleph**, the airy or aetherial element that surrounds the Cube.

Aleph is traditionally allocated to the element of Air and is a consonant that has no sound. It is rather like the tiny pause represented by the hyphen in a word like "re-open." In relation to the Cube of Space it is the space where creation can happen, where God can manifest, midway between the principle of archetypal Spirit and the principle of archetypal Water.

Then come the seven "double" letters, and each one belongs symbolically to one of the six faces of the cube plus its centre.

The remaining twelve "single" letters are allocated to the twelve edges of the cube. Thus in the Cube of Space we have a symbol based on the mystical numbers 3, 7 and 12, also represented by the three pillars of the Tree of Life, the seven traditional planets and the twelve signs of the zodiac.

We have described this composite symbol at some length in *Experience of the Inner Worlds* (Skylight Press 2010.)

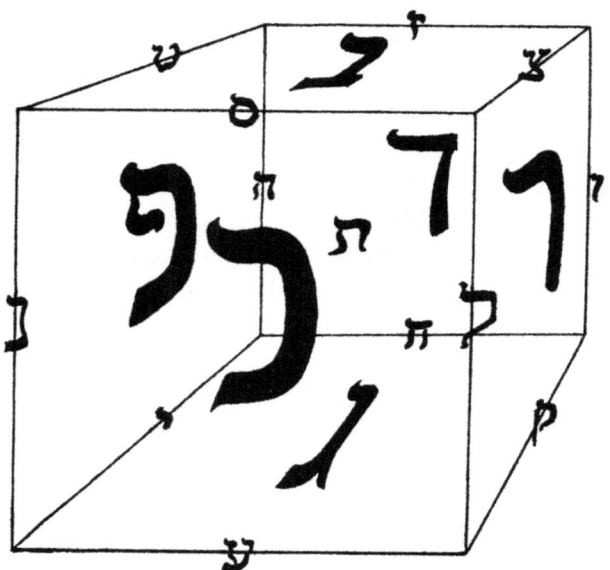

Figure 8: The Cube of Space

In its original conception it was an attempt to show how God used certain basic principles of number to form the creation. In this kind of approach to God, not thinking of Him as a great potentate, but approaching Him as a benevolent father, as holder of the balance and thus creator of beauty, we get to the idea of God behind the three middle Sephiroth on the Tree of Life: Chesed, Geburah and Tiphareth.

The next great literary out-pouring of the Qabalah was in 1305 when a Spanish Jew known as Moses de León produced the *Zohar*, or Book of Splendour. This is what our own Gentile Qabalism is based upon, even though most of us have never read it.

There is a translation available which is worth looking at if only to show how different our conception as 20th century occult-minded Gentiles is from 14th century mystical Jews. Again, they are very much concerned with God, largely through an analysis of His word, and what it really meant. Much of the first volume of the *Zohar* is just concerned with the first sentence in Genesis, and commences with a lengthy analysis of its first word, Bereshith – even spending a lot of time on the first letter.

This is because they believed that language was sacred, and their own language in particular was that of God. For this reason they exploited all kinds of coding to find hidden meanings in the Bible.

Moses de León wrote this huge work in Aramaic, for he said it was written by Simeon ben Jochai, the traditional author of the *Sepher Yetzirah*. It seems reasonable to assume that Moses de León wrote down what was an oral tradition, for it plainly has the work of many minds behind it. Within it there is the Tree of Life, also a certain amount of low magic, character reading from physiognomy for example, but above all, a very intense speculative mysticism including minute analysis of Biblical texts.

Let us take the first word of the first sentence of Genesis, for example, which is by no means so cut and dried as to meaning as the English translation might suggest. In the original Hebrew, for instance, it is difficult to sort out what is object and what is subject. It refers to God as Elohim, which is a feminine stem on a masculine plural ending. Literally one could say it means "the gods who created the world" and that they were male and female. However, that is not quite correct because the real creativity implied is that in the beginning "the un-nameable" created "the gods." Now who or what are the gods that were created? If we were to coin modern terms, perhaps the archetypes of the unconscious? But that is limiting them. They could be called devas, angels, spirits.

All this kind of Qabalistic speculation is more "down to earth" than the Cube of Space. It is how God actually works through creatures of the inner worlds or of the outer worlds; how He manifests His glory; how He obtains His victory at the Last Trump when creation is called back into Himself. It is how He, like Atlas, holds up the whole world; how His is the foundation of the world, of the laws of science. All this pertains to the lower Sephiroth of Netzach, Hod and Yesod, whose attributes are Glory, Victory and the Foundation.

It is with Malkuth that we get more to modern times, with our Gentile misinterpretation, which does, however, have its own validity. It has been called highly coloured nonsense. To a Jewish mystic it might well seem so, just as, to a rather blinkered modern occultist, medieval Jewish mysticism may sound nonsense. But it is, to either party, a great loss if they cannot understand the other's point of view, because what we have in fact is God creating a universe which has an outer aspect and an inner aspect.

Thus we can investigate three things. We can be material scientists, artists or technologists who concern ourselves entirely with the outer creation. Or we can be inner scientists, artists or technologists who concern ourselves with the inside of creation. And one can do this without any reference to God at all, at any rate up to a certain point.

Just as an outer scientist can be completely godless so an inner scientist can be completely godless, although experience suggests that they either see the light sooner or later, or else manifest some rather unfortunate results in their lives, usually in the form of gross inflation of the personality.

The third element is God. One could concern oneself with God, as a complete mystic, renouncing the world in a total concern with God. Most of us do not go to these lengths. We live life in the world and come to terms with God as best we may.

There are certain of us who are principally interested in the inner worlds, and we also have to take God into account. At first we may not have to, but the more we get into the inner worlds the more important this becomes. Otherwise one may be fishing with one's little rod and line and will get a fish on the end of it that will be rather bigger than one bargained for. It might well prove to be of God. It could also be demonic.

An interesting watershed occurs in the 17th century. Let us, in Figure 9, examine a diagram Robert Fludd conceived. We see

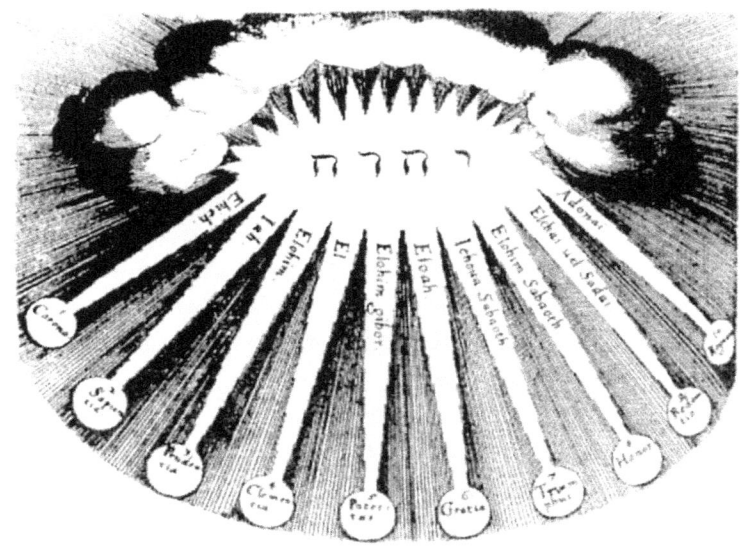

Figure 9: The Divine Emanations

that he is concerned with the Jewish Qabalah, and it is still very much to do with God. There is God, JHVH, coming out of a cloud, and there in the Sephiroth are all the ways He manifests Himself – all at once. The Crown of Wisdom, Prudence, Mercy, Power, Grace, Triumph, Honour, Redemption, the Kingdom. This cloud formation is a favourite convention of Fludd's and also of the Rosicrucians. They are very fond of the phrase "Under the shadow of Thy wings, Jehovah" and this is what Fludd is showing here.

Jehovah is the most holy name of God. No Jew is allowed to pronounce that name. In fact that is how we have got the name Jehovah. Those four consonants really have no consonantal sound at all. They are aspirant consonants as can be judged when modern scholars refer to Jehovah as Yahweh – that is, *Ee-ah-oo-ay*. In intention it is rather like the Eastern word Au-uu-m or Om. It is a name structured out of vowels. From this perhaps we get the idea behind the phrase "the letter killeth but the spirit giveth life." The consonants are the letters and are unpronounceable unless we put vowels in between them. This is another symbolic way of showing God acting through the creation. The creation is represented by the consonants and the spirit of God by the vowels. The spirit and the breath were originally synonymous words.

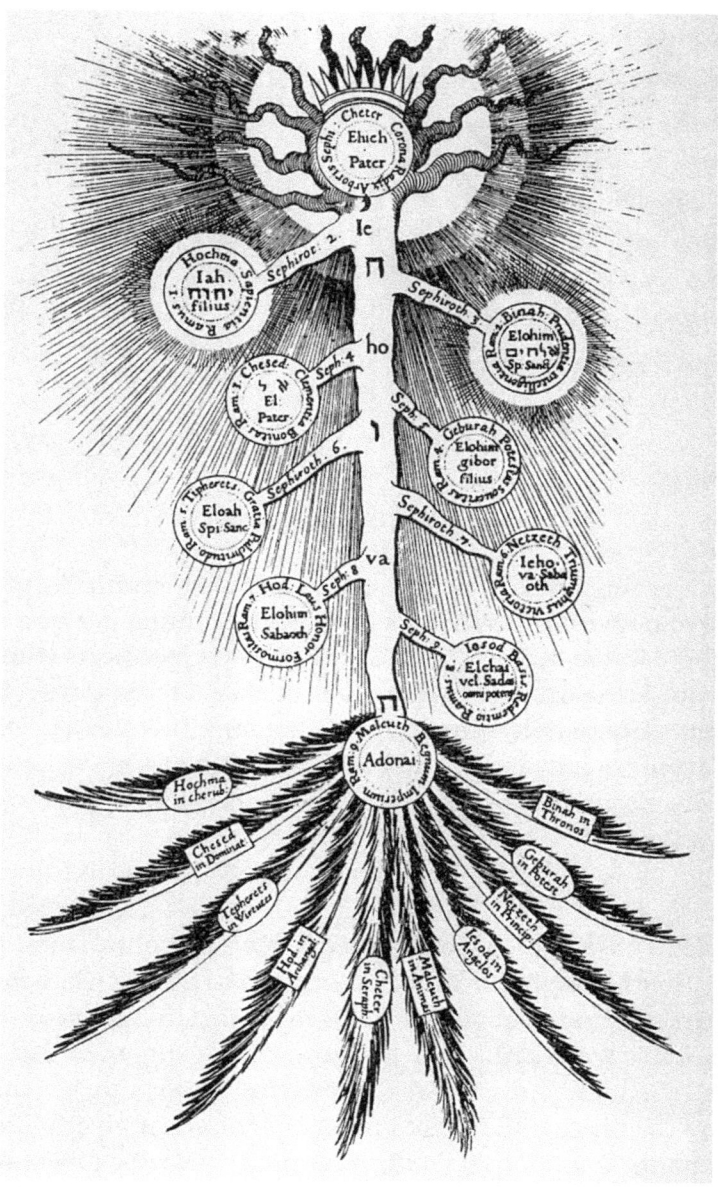

Figure 10: The Tree of Life in Root and Branch

A devout Jew reading his Bible, when he came to JHVH would say "Adonai", which means Lord. In the original Hebrew text there were just consonants. Points to indicate the vowels were added later, after a few centuries, to help people. And although JHVH remain consonants on the page, the vowel pointings used were the pointings for Adonai. The translators into English did not realise this and so they used consonants with the wrong vowel pointing, which gave them the name Jehovah.

Another version of the Tree of Life by Fludd in Figure 10 is rather more like a Tree. It has some interesting aspects. The roots are in God Himself, and God emerges like a blossoming tree from His own root. To represent the creation, at the lowest level, are feathers, that are emblematic of the choirs of angels.

So we are a long way from the Earth when talking about Malkuth here. We are talking about God as creator and ruler and director of all the choirs of angels. The Cherubim, the Dominions, the Virtues, Archangels, Principalities, Powers, Thrones. Each with their own function, as guides of individuals, or guides of groups, or guides of nations, or guardians of intellectual and moral principles. And here we see Fludd again very much with the conception that the Qabalah is entirely a description of God – and not of His creation.

One further diagram, in Figure 11, does however give an interesting link between the Tree of Life as image of God, and as

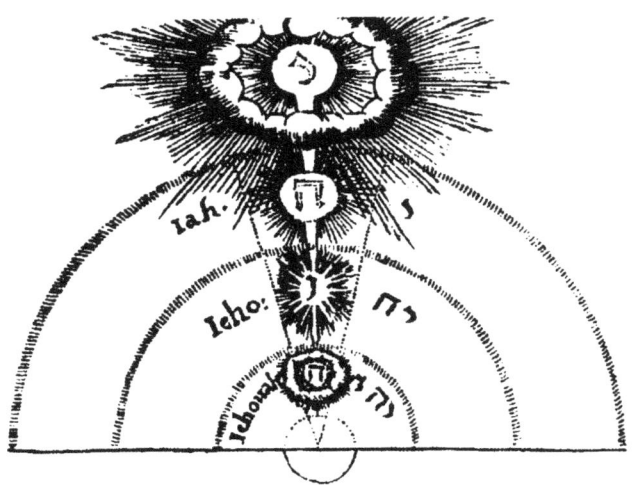

Figure 11: The Expression of the Holy Name

image of the creation. This is a development of the Holy Name, but this time showing how God concerns Himself with more detailed aspects of the creation.

This diagram is rather like a half circle of the full circle of Figure 6 where God is completely surrounding the creation and coming in to hold everything within Himself. Here we have first of all the Yod, the first seed or hand of God, dynamic power, and then a concreting down into Ya, Yehoh, Yehovah.

Associated with this, in Figure 12, is an interesting diagram of a man, that develops the Biblical text that God created man in His own image. It shows God on the one hand, and on the other, man with his spirit, the focus of which is above his head; his intellect; his vita or vital spark, and his natural faculties or physical perceptions.

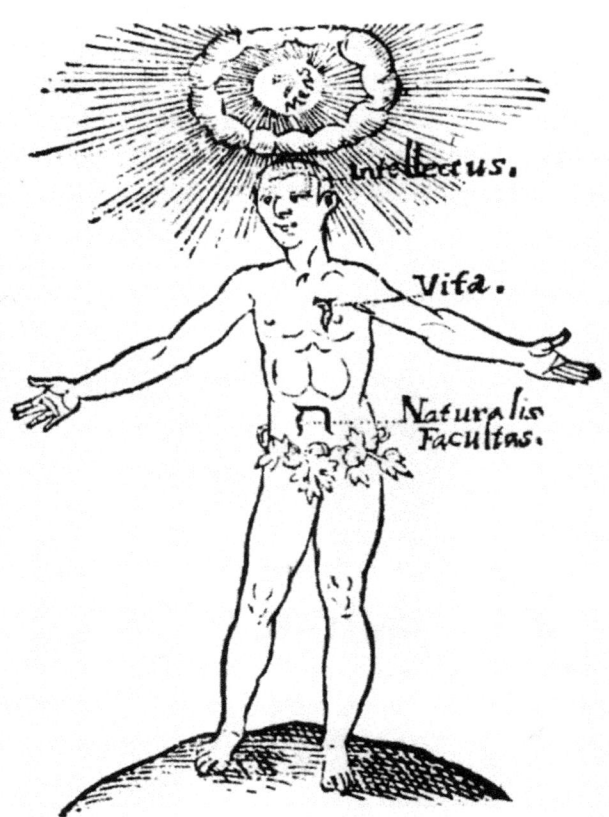

Figure 12: Man in the Image of God

It was by this mode of thought that the gentile Qabalists of the Renaissance, through to our own time, saw a relation between God and his creation through man, as God's image.

What has happened in our rather materialistic age is that most people who are interested in inner science, or the occult, have become divorced from, or out of communication with informed theological thought. Thus God has tended to be forgotten about, and we arrive at an analysis of the inner dynamics of creation with God either ignored, or else reduced to a kind of tenuous interstellar gas: the Primal Nothingness. We refer to Him in very bleak abstractions. He is physical but very very simple and diffuse, almost like interstellar hydrogen. We have made God into hydrogen.

Of course hydrogen may blow us up in the end – which could serve us right. An ironic twist of karma there, if one likes to think of it in that way. We reduce our conception of God to that of interstellar hydrogen, and then blow ourselves up with hydrogen bombs!

Originally published in Quadriga 12: Winter 1979

4

the tree of life as model of the universe

A BOOK first published in 1863/4 by Ginsburg, called *The Essenes and the Qabalah* remains a very good historical summary of the Jewish movements in early Qabalistic thought.

Many people do not realise that there is also a tremendous amount of Qabalistic literature in Hebrew which has never been translated, and the Qabalah that we talk about today is a tiny fraction of the whole literature. Furthermore, the actual Jewish Qabalah is very much a mystical literature, and in this respect is different from the Gentile tradition, which combines scientific tradition with the mystical and goes back to the ancient Greeks and Egyptians.

In fact a great deal of the esoteric tradition which many people today regard as Qabalistic is not Jewish at all but was ancient Greek and then Christian tradition before the Qabalah was ever heard of in the West. It will be instructive to see how these two strands came together.

The key person is Marsilio Ficino, who was a scholar and translator, priest and physician, who worked for the Borgia family. At that time Italy was divided into small principalities, some of which patronised the arts and scholarly work. Ficino's job in the court was to translate classical Greek texts which were then being discovered.

In this Renaissance period Christendom was just coming out of its introversion and discovering that there was a great classical world that had existed before Christ; and also discovering, with some amazement, that it had been a very high civilisation. Marsilio

Ficino was translating the works of Plato, but was asked to stop translating Plato because something even more important had come up: the scripts of Hermes.

Hermes was thought to be an ancient Egyptian priest. His work was very much along the lines of what we call esotericism. There was much high speculation about the inner worlds in it, together with quite a lot of low magic. In fact it is a collection of scripts by many hands which were written between the 1st and 3rd century AD, when the high traditions of pagan spirituality met in confluence with the rising Christian religion. A number of philosophers of the time tried to amalgamate the insights of Christianity with the insights of the pagan world.

When these scripts came into Renaissance Europe in 1450 however, it was thought that they had been written by an Egyptian priest who was contemporary with Moses. Therefore even the church itself regarded the Hermetic scripts as very important because they obliquely mentioned the coming of Christianity. On the assumption that they were written by a contemporary of Moses this looked like prophecy. So the church regarded Hermes as an enlightened pagan, a non-Jew who had yet been sufficiently close to God to have been vouchsafed with foreknowledge of the Incarnation.

Marsilio Ficino therefore started translation of these Hermetic texts. A large part of them was concerned with how objects in the world are related to the stars and particularly the planets.

This, in fact, is not so much original to Hermes as part of ancient Greek science, which can be traced to Aristotle in many cases. Aristotle was regarded very highly in the Middle Ages, and a lot of the church's attitude to the natural world was based on his writings. The great doctors of the church, principally Thomas Aquinas, and his great teacher, Albertus Magnus, filled in the great cultural gaps that had arisen during the barbarian dark ages by reconciling Christian theology with Greek science.

Part of Greek science which was a feature of the Hermetic scripts was the doctrine of correspondences. In its broadest sense it is a vehicle of high philosophy: that which is below is as that which is above; the earth is a mirror of the heavens; to investigate the inner worlds look to the outer world; man's art and science are a putting a mirror to nature.

It can also be used in a lower, more piecemeal fashion as the doctrine of signatures in the operations of science, particularly medicine. Thus to cure fever or prickling sensations in disease the best place to look for a cure or cause might be a prickly bush such as holly or thistle. All the various flowers and herbs had their planetary relationships, as did the parts of the human body. Thus the whole of the natural universe was looked upon as a system of relationships.

Ficino started to experiment along these lines. He reasoned that if a scholar spent a lot of time in the library and became pasty faced and turgid it was because there was too much of Saturn and Mercury in his occupation. To counterbalance this he should concentrate on the powers of Venus and the Sun, perhaps by going out on sunny days and admiring the beauty of flowers.

This is, of course, the very simple beginnings of nature therapy or a commonsense balanced way of life. He went on from there, however, to wonder if it might be possible also to counterbalance the effects of an unfortunate astrological configuration.

He set aside a room and placed within it lamps to represent the different planets. These could be moved around into more congenial positions whilst he sat in the middle of this "corrected" astrological chart. He also composed what he called Orphic Hymns, on the foundations of ancient Greek literature, hymns to Venus, hymns to Jupiter, and so on, and also a symbolic system of musical notation the better to help counterbalance the unfortunate astrological influences.

Although this attracted the sympathetic interest of more than one Pope of the time, Ficino realised that he was treading on very thin theological ice. He therefore took pains to insist that he was only concerned with natural magic, that is to say, with objects in the natural world and how they are related to the stars.

Now the physical world is part of God's creation and the stars also are part of God's creation. The stars may be pushed around by angels, as was believed at the time, but they are still part of the creation. And Ficino was most concerned to point out that in this natural magic he was not in any way concerned with trying to influence the angels to manipulate the stars in a different way. One accepted the way the angels, under direction from God, moved the stars around, but it was quite legitimate by natural means of the doctrine of signatures to ameliorate their effects.

So far this has little to do with the Qabalah. Marsilio Ficino was a Greek scholar and knew nothing about the Qabalah. Even though *The Zohar* had been around for 150 years, it was written in Aramaic, which is a kind of common language corruption of classical Hebrew.

There was, however, a Renaissance prince of great culture and brilliance, Pico della Mirandola, who could read Hebrew and Aramaic. He had read *The Zohar,* and at the age of 24 turned up in Rome announcing that he had a great new philosophy derived from the Jewish Qabalah. He very much wanted to interest the Pope in it as a means of converting the Jews to Christianity. According to the way that Pico read and understood *The Zohar,* Christianity could be proved from it.

Now of course the Qabalistic scholar Professor Scholem and orthodox Jews would consider this a complete misunderstanding on Pico's part, but on the Tree of Life one has all these threes, which of course Pico related to the Holy Trinity. He therefore developed a system of philosophy showing how the Trinitarian God could be understood by the secret tradition of the Jews.

Just as the Jews, although the chosen people of the Old Testament, had not understood the coming of the Christ and had rejected him, so did they have this marvellous secret tradition which they themselves did not understand. Pico considered that with Christian enlightenment one could understand, and that there was a Christian interpretation plainly to see.

This met with mixed reactions because Pico was not satisfied only with this, but linked it with Marsilio Ficino's experiments in natural magic. In Ficino's natural magic we have all the correspondences that objects in the natural world have with the planets, to which Pico della Mirandola's Qabalah adds corresponding choirs of angels and their correspondence with certain Holy Names of God. Thus by invoking these Holy Names of God one can influence the angels which in turn influence the planets which can influence the lower world. This created a furore because the implications are very considerable indeed.

Members of the church hierarchy were horrified when Pico went on to suggest that the miracles of Jesus were done by Qabalistic magic; they saw that church authority in all matters spiritual was likely to be eroded by the Qabalistic philosophers, magicians and scientists. Pico had a difficult time. The Inquisition condemned him and he was imprisoned for some time for heresy, though was later released. Alternate Popes in this intellectually turbulent period were either for him or against him.

In 1539 *The Zohar* was first published in Latin, the translation of Knorr von Rosenrath. It is part of that translation that MacGregor Mathers rendered into English as *The Kabbalah Unveiled*. We have moved on quite a bit from the Tree of Life seen as God.

We now have it on four levels:

- We have the Tree of Life in the Jewish conception as God and His ways of revealing Himself.

- Then there is the next level of it, which is the Lord God, Adonai, as commander and creator of the angels, the angels being the spiritual powers who keep the universe going.

- The third level is of the stars we see about us which are pushed about by the angels.

- The final level is the Qabalah of the correspondences of the metals, flowers, plants, parts of the human body and the rest of the natural physical world.

We have the elements of a complete science, inner and outer, stretching from God, through the angels, through the inner mechanics of the psychic side of existence, down to the physical reality. This is the doctrine known as the Four Worlds of the Qabalists.

The highest world, the world of **Atziluth**, is all the Sephiroth seen as God (Figure 13). That world is God.

The next one down is the Creative World, called **Briah**, which consists of the choirs of angels. This again was part of Christian tradition, and again, like the Hermetic scripts, originating in the 2nd or 3rd century AD as a confluence of pagan with Christian insights.

An unknown philosopher wrote a book called *The Celestial Hierarchies* under the name of Dionysius. This was assumed by Medieval and Renaissance men to be Dionysius the Areopogite who is mentioned in the New Testament as a close friend of St. Paul. Therefore this book of the celestial hierarchies, which was a treatise on angels, was considered to be almost of equal authority as the

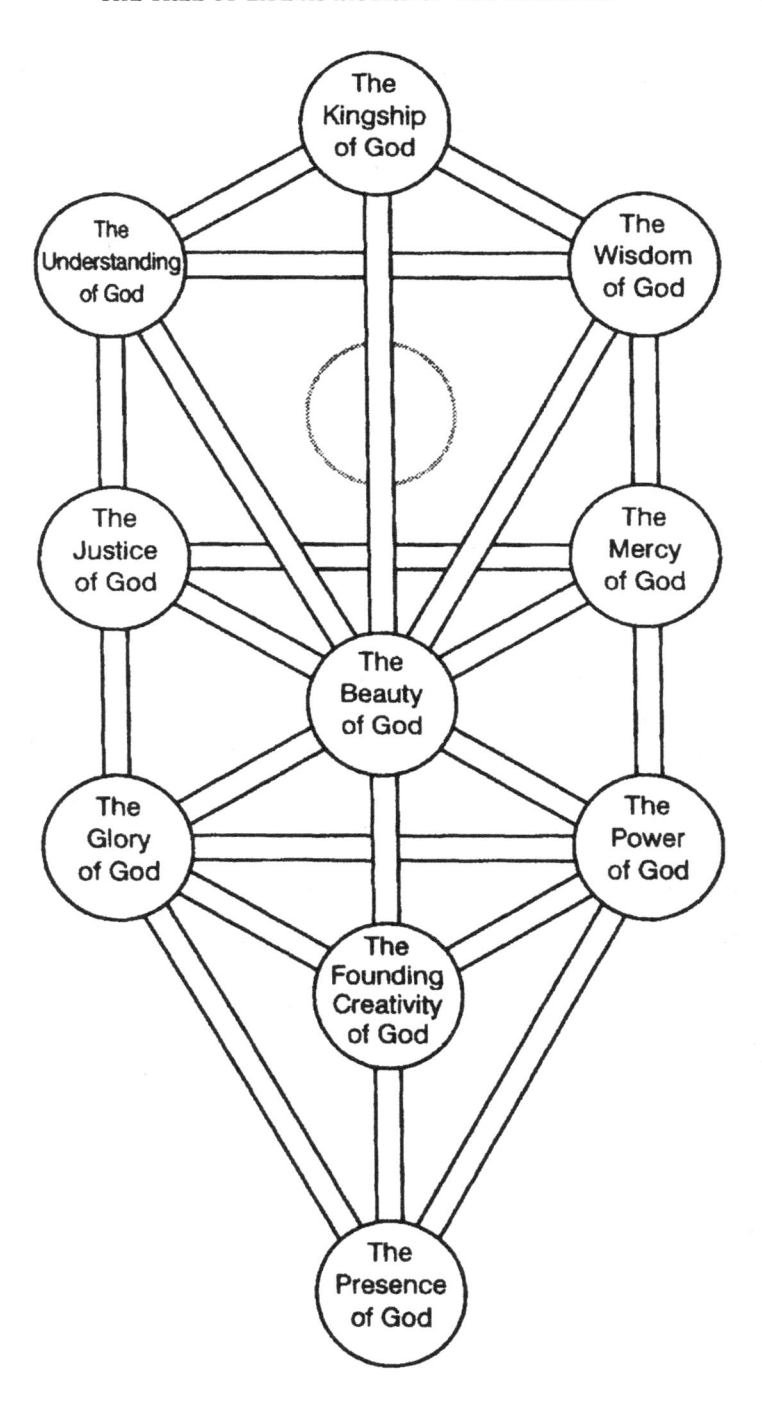

Figure 13: The Tree of Life in the Archetypal World
showing attributes of God

New Testament, and was accorded considerable respect by the church. This was grafted on to the Hebrew angelic system.

There are various nomenclatures for the angelic choirs. Dionysius' version is not quite the same as in the Qabalistic Jewish tradition, but the differences are largely superficial, and we can use the diagram of the Tree of Life to describe them (Figure 14).

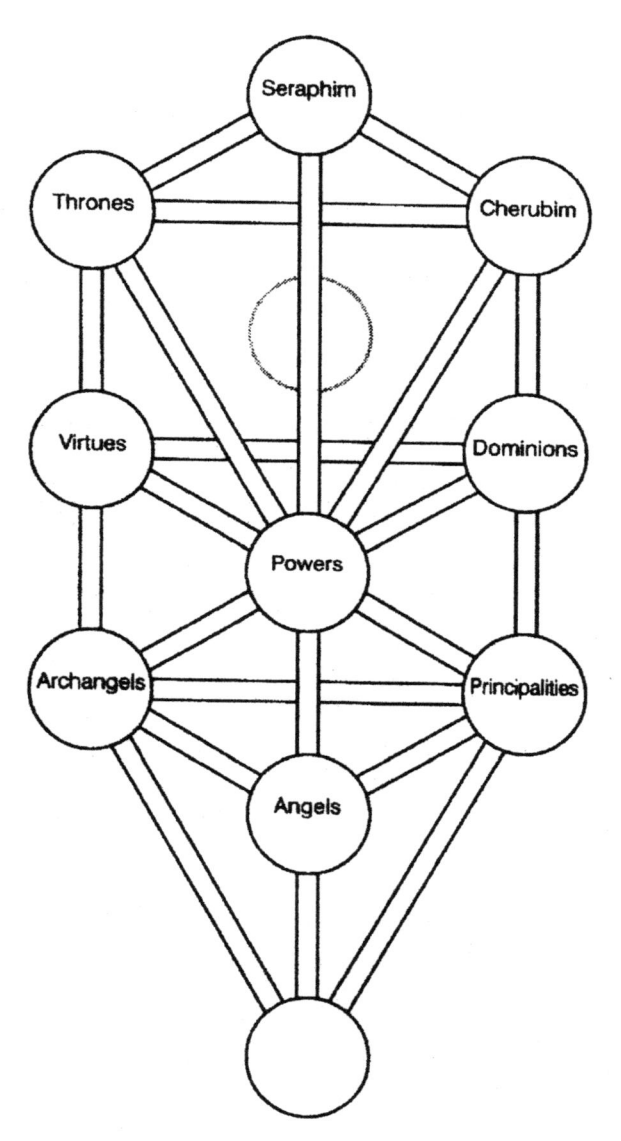

Figure 14: The Tree of Life in the Creative World showing Angelic Choirs

THE TREE OF LIFE AS MODEL OF THE UNIVERSE

There are nine orders of angels in three principal groups of which the highest is composed of Seraphim, Cherubim and Thrones. These exist face to face with God, and the Seraphim reflect the order the providence of God, the Cherubim the essence and form of God, whilst the Thrones also, on occasion, descend to do specific works of God.

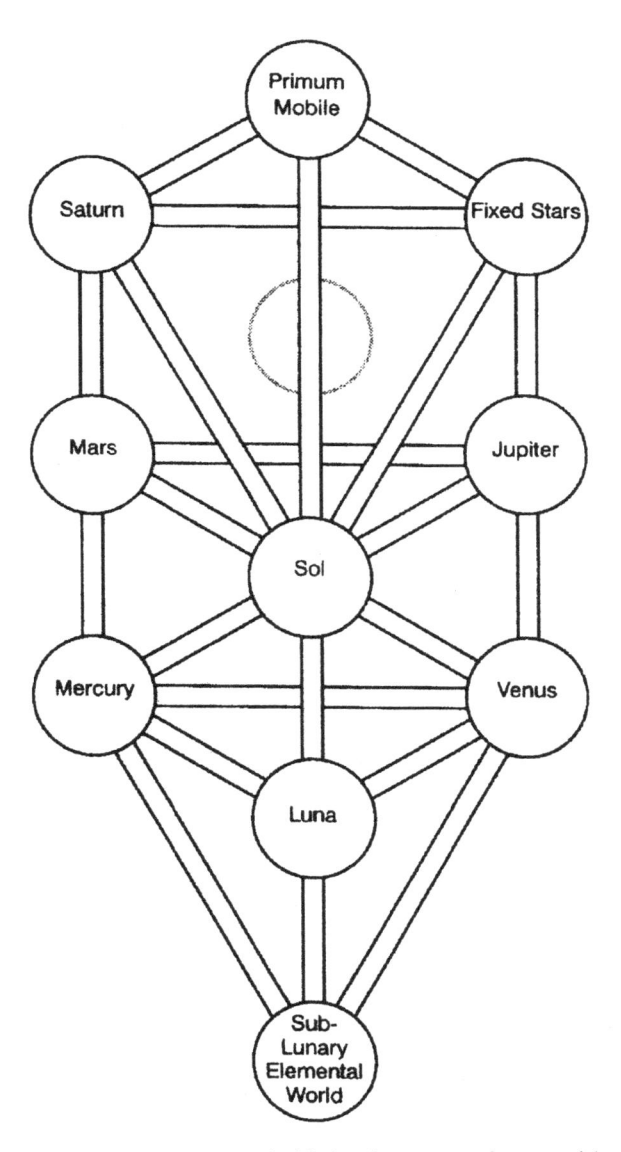

Figure 15: The Tree of Life in the Formative World showing Planetary Spheres

The next group of three are the Dominions, the Virtues and Powers. The Dominions are the architects of the universe, they design what the others execute. The Virtues are the ones who move the heavens; the executors of destiny on a macrocosmic scale. The Powers watch the order of divine governance to see that it is not interrupted, and some of them may descend to communicate with

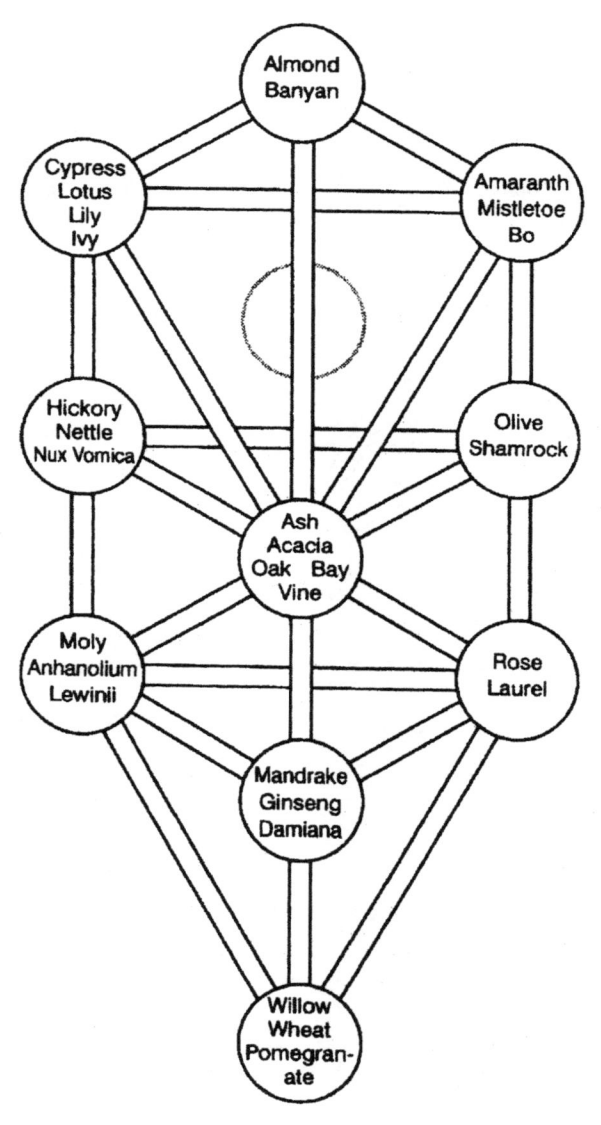

Figure 16: The Tree of Life in the Material World showing representative Plants

human beings. It will be realised however that in the normal way we do not have a great deal of concourse with these higher orders.

Of the three lower orders, Principalities care for public affairs, nations, rulers and human government in the wider sense; they are the racial angels and angels of large groups and nations. Archangels are concerned with the worship and different religions of man, whilst the Angels are concerned with individuals, so that is where your "good angel" will be.

So much for the world of angels. At the next level we have the Sun, Moon, and planets of the celestial Tree, and the Formative World of the Qabalah, **Yetzirah** (Figure 15). There are the five planets visible to the naked eye, the Earth, the sphere of the fixed stars, and then the Primum Mobile, the clear crystal sphere which keeps everything going.

They correspond with the Sephiroth of the Tree of Life and one can work on one's own psychology by meditating upon them as did Marsilio Ficino. Some of the paintings of his contemporary Botticelli we think are probably magical diagrams for this purpose. The one of Venus rising from the sea is a famous one and certainly could be used as a magical image for meditation upon the powers of Venus.

The lowest of the Four Worlds of the Qabalists is the Material World, called **Assiah**, in which are all the objects of the natural world, classified according to planetary correspondences in Renaissance encyclopaedic works such as Cornelius Agrippa's *De Occulta Philosophia* (Figure 16).

It is possible – although it can be a source of confusion – to put up the Four Worlds on one single Tree of Life (Figure 17). The highest, archetypal world could be related to Kether; the Creative World of the angels to Binah and Chokmah; the Formative World to Tiphareth and its surrounding Sephiroth, and the physical world to Malkuth.

This is a useful device but we have to remember that there should be four Trees of Life. That is, there is a Tree of itself in Atziluth, which is God. Then there is a similar Tree in Briah, which is the angelic one. There is then a Tree related to the planets and the inner worlds, which is the Yetziratic Tree. Finally there is a Tree of physical correspondences which is the Tree in Assiah, the material world.

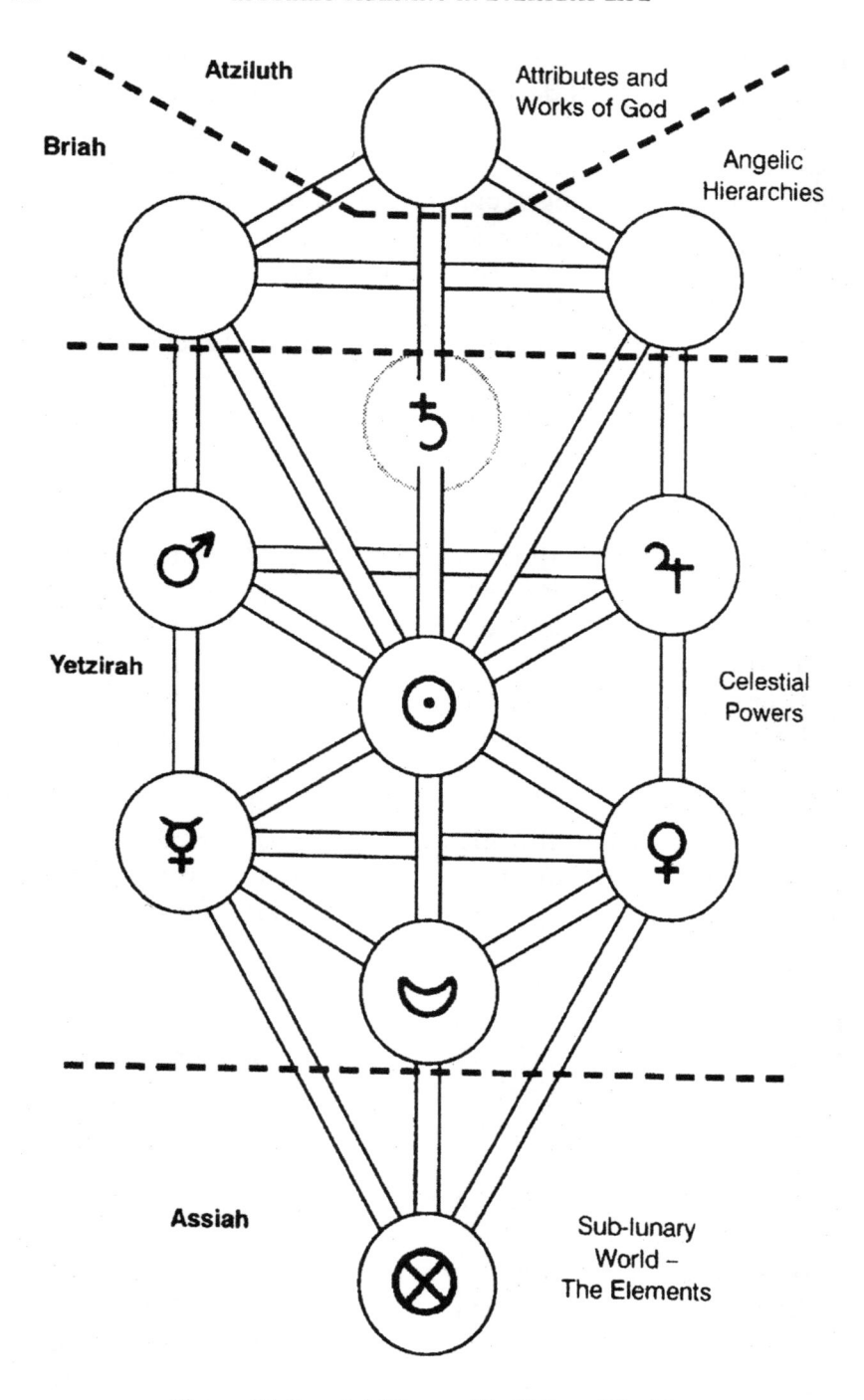

Figure 17: Fourfold Tree with all Four Worlds

We ought to be a little more specific than we often are about which Tree we are dealing with in any particular case. Otherwise what tends to happen is that the 4 in 1 Tree is used as a vehicle for teaching that God is in Kether, Malkuth is the Earth, with consciousness taking up the spheres in between. That is an over-simplification to the point of distortion. In fact the whole fourfold Tree has to be taken into account, first from Kether to Malkuth as ten aspects of God; following on that, the orders of angels; at the next level the celestial correspondences; and at the lowest level the physical correspondences: four Trees.

Marsilio Ficino, when he was playing his viola da gamba with his coloured lights singing to the stars was operating on the two lower Trees. The original mystical Qabalah of the Jews was concerned almost entirely with the Tree in Atziluth, to a lesser extent with the Tree in Briah. When Pico della Mirandola put all four together it had quite important consequences.

Let us examine an example of this fourfold world picture in a diagram by Robert Fludd (Figure 18). Fludd is very useful to us as he links the ancient conceptions of inner science with our modern ones.

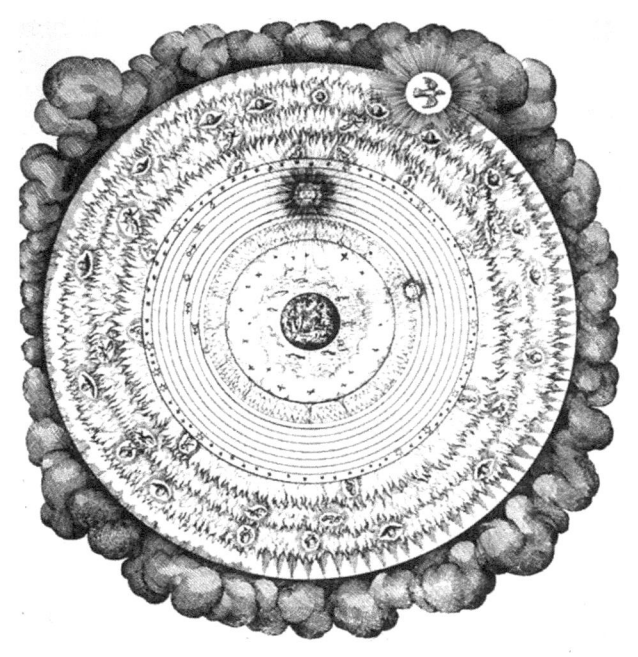

Figure 18: The Heavens and Earth, after Robert Fludd

We described the Jewish mystical conception of God creating a Void within Himself. Fludd shows this by the dove of the Holy Spirit, which has flown round in a complete circle to create a space within God, within which He can then create. Then within this fiery trail formed by the Holy Spirit we have three sets of circles in which are the nine angelic choirs, Seraphim, Cherubim, Dominions, Thrones, Powers, Principalities, Virtues, Archangels and Angels. There they all are. God has created them and they are all looking in upon the lower creation, the great crystalline sphere in which all the heavens are contained. And within that crystalline sphere are other spheres. There is the sphere of all the fixed stars that we see when we look at the sky. Its axis is the Pole Star, which seems to be static, with the rest of the stars revolving round it.

There are seven other heavenly bodies which move on wandering paths, each with its own sphere. These are the planets Saturn, Jupiter, Mars, the Sun, Venus, Mercury and the Moon, all circling about the Earth.

The idea of all these bodies revolving round the Earth may seem to have been disproved by Copernicus but the physical scientific viewpoint is here an irrelevance. This diagram of Robert Fludd shows the universe as it is viewed by ourselves, by man. And for our purposes, the point of view of evolving consciousness, it is the only valid way of looking at the universe. Each one of us is at the centre of the universe. This is a matter for common observation. Each one of us is a spiritual centre about which the objective world turns. To lose sight of this fact is to become a mere object in someone else's universe. It follows that it is quite valid to look upon the earth as the centre of the universe as far as the human race is concerned.

In the centre of all are the Four Elements, of which everything is made. Earth and Water are the two basic solid elements with the element of Air around them. Encircling them is a ring of Fire, which is about where science now puts the stratosphere.

In another famous picture by Fludd, engraved by de Bruy, *The Mirror of the Whole of Nature and the Image of Art* (Figure 19), Nature is represented by a naked female figure; Art, which includes Science, by a monkey; and God by the name JHVH in a cloud with a hand coming from it. God is not in the creation but outside it, symbolically in a cloud, and then come the outer circles with orders of angels who control the destinies of the created worlds, followed by a narrow clear space which is the primum mobile, and then a circle of stars of the starry heavens, and then in turn, spheres of Saturn, Jovis, Mars, the Sun, Venus, Mercury and the Moon. These are the crystalline spheres.

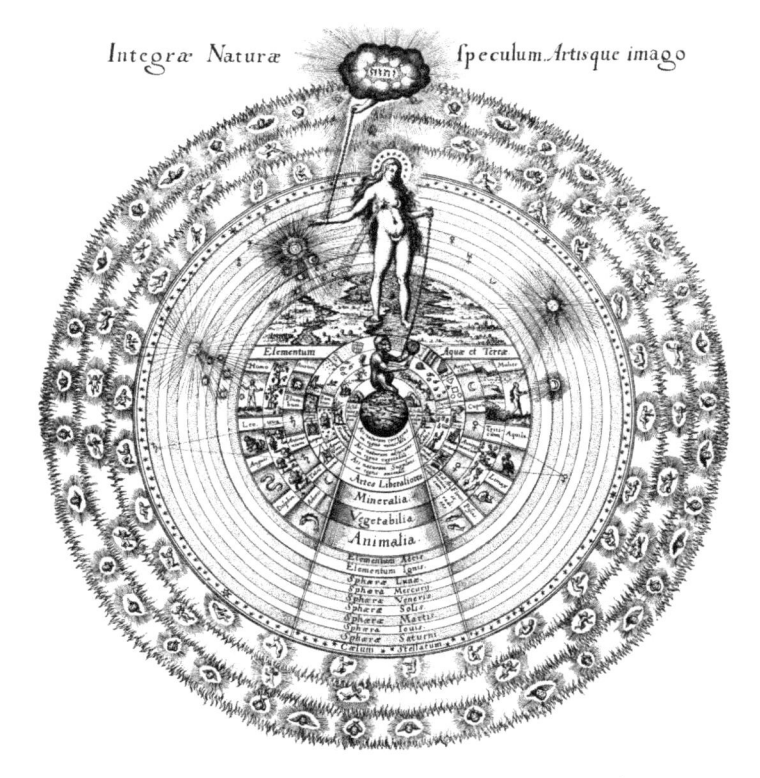

Figure 19: The Mirror of Nature and Image of Art

The crystal spheres all relate to spheres on the Tree of Life, from the Primum Mobile in Kether, and the Fixed Stars in Chokmah, down to Malkuth the Earth. In the centre we have first of all, inside the Sphere of the Moon, the element of Fire, a fiery belt around the Earth, our cordon sanitaire, then the element of Air, and inside that a complicated structure to represent the elements of Water and Earth and all that resides therein. The outer sphere contains animals, going from the bottom left there is a dolphin, snake, lion, man, and then going round the other side, woman, eagle, snail and two fish. These are representatives of different parts of the animal creation. For the full implications of Fludd's particular symbolism one would have to read Fludd's Latin text. It is interesting to note that the man is turned towards the Sun and the woman is facing the Moon.

The next circle is the vegetable, where we have examples of trees, grapes, flowers and roots. Fludd probably does have some symbolic significance in mind, in that grapes make wine, and wheat makes bread.

Then inside these are the minerals, and the examples he has, going in a clockwise direction, are talc, antimony, lead, gold, silver, copper, auripigmentum.

You may also notice some lines of correspondence drawn in. On the crystalline spheres of Venus, from the planet Venus, are two little lines going to show that Venus is related to copper and to auripigmentum. On the other side, the symbol for the planet Saturn has correspondences drawn through to join up with lead and antimony. Plainly if Fludd were to try to draw in every correspondence it would have been an impossibly complex diagram but he shows one or two examples to give the general idea. This is the world as constituted physically in the view of mankind until very recently.

Within this creation there is the world of nature, which is the naked female figure, the form of Isis, if one likes to use the pagan terminology. Fludd's description of her is worth quoting: "She is not a goddess but the proximate minister of God at whose behest she governs the sub-celestial worlds."

Thus she is a hand-maiden of God who governs the natural world. As a 17th century Anglican, Robert Fludd was rather chary about giving her goddess status but I do not think we need be quite so cautious; much depends on how one defines the term goddess.

He goes on to explain: "In the picture she is joined to God by a chain which descends through all the hierarchy of existence. She is the Soul of the World or the invisible fire of Heraclitus and Zoroaster. It is she who turns the sphere of the stars and disposes the planetary influences to the elemental realms nourishing all creatures from her bosom."

She therefore seems to be a being, or principle, comprised of the ruling work of all the angels; or a personification of inner nature, *natura naturans*, acting on behalf of God. God being the architect, the planner, she being the mediatrix, the one who puts everything into operation.

"On her breast is the true Sun." This I think we can regard as the spiritual sun behind the sun. "On her belly the moon. Her heart gives light to the stars and planets, whose influence, infused in her womb, called by the philosophers the spirit of the moon, is sent down to the very centre of the earth." This reminds me of some work with an early group of mine in Tewkesbury from 1965-70 where we had workings given through which were related to bringing forces down from a high interstellar temple down to the centre of the earth; and this pattern has been resumed from time to time in various work since then. It is therefore interesting to see Fludd referring to the importance of bringing forces down to the centre of the earth when he is talking about the Isis of Nature.

"Her right foot stands on earth, her left in water, signifying the conjunction of sulphur and mercury without which nothing can be created." These are the principles of positive and negative familiar to most students of esoteric philosophy.

This female figure is very important to us if we are inner scientists, or psychics, or magicians, for we are really priests and priestesses of Isis, or cooperators with the soul of the world, working under God. In fact we should not be too esoteric or sectarian about this function. We are all part of the human race and in spite of a great artificial divide that has built up there is nothing that separates inner from outer scientists or artists.

We, along with them, are part of Fludd's monkey. This has nothing to do with Darwin's theory of evolution; in Fludd's time the monkey was seen first and foremost as imitator, not ancestor, and the monkey shows this imitative principle in man; the whole of man's science in this view being the examination of nature and the attempt to copy it. It is a matter for the philosopher of science whether in fact we improve on nature or whether we do not. Some of our machinery, our technology, certainly can do things which nature cannot. On the other hand there are things in nature which man's technology cannot imitate. Whether we shall succeed in doing so, who knows?

Certainly the earlier scientists did not share our modern assumption that the world is man's oyster that he may exploit to the limits of his intelligence and rapacity, with technology simply a slave and tool in doing this.

The early scientists were very much concerned with demonstrating the greater glory of God as revealed in nature. Robert Boyle for instance used the analogy of a fly's eye as proof of the existence of God because there is so much design and technology in the eye of that tiny creature which completely outclasses man's grasp of optics and physics. Who designed the eye of a fly? The same argument applies to another favourite example of theirs, the paw of a dog. One can take almost anything in nature and there find evidence of intelligence and creation. Man has only just begun to apply this himself, and how we apply it is a matter of some importance as to whether we survive as a race.

Since Fludd's day, science has been looking more and more intensively at the material world, copying it, trying to improve upon it, and our life is based on scientific tools and toys, from electric light and cars to dynamite and machine guns. We learn from nature and then we use our intelligence to apply what we have learned. Many intellectual problems have been solved, but they tend to throw up some difficult moral ones as man strives to become more and more "as God" in power if not in love and wisdom.

Originally published in Quadriga 16: Winter 1980

5

reflections on life and spirituality

Celebration of the Forces of Life

LIFE AS expressed on Earth has four phases according to the Seasons – Spring, Summer, Autumn, Winter. It is also expressed at four levels of complexity – mineral, vegetable, animal and human. We can join the two in a series of linked meditations, which are not so much a going inside our own heads, but a contemplative observation of what is going on in life outside us.

In Spring, the time when the seeds start to sprout forth their potential roots and flowers, let us contemplate a few actual seeds – be they sunflower, dandelion, onion or what you will. Look at each one (and the physical act is important, this is not a mere mental exercise) and try to become aware of the whole plant that is held within it – powers and forms that have their origin on the etheric plane, which gives form to physical life.

In Summer turn your contemplation to the animal kingdom, be it your pet cat or dog, or horses and cows in the fields. In the same way that the inner world of the plant could be discerned by contemplation of the seed, so may the angelic oversoul of the animal kingdoms be astrally contacted through the animal you confront.

In Autumn take cognisance of the human world, and the works of man, in the patterns of towns and cities and inventions. Those patterns show the inner pattern of the spirit of man, striving to express, often in incomplete or misconceived ways, the principles of civilisation. Principles that obviously have not been fully worked out at this stage in the evolution of the world. But rather than despair at the follies and errors so expressed, take a reverential and positive view of the persistence and indomitable nature of the human spirit despite all adversities. Let love shine through, and compassion, for the evil doer as well as the afflicted, for both are opposite sides of the same human coin.

And in Winter, complete the cycle with contemplation of the ground base of Earth, the mineral world. Take a crystal, or a metal, for all metals have a crystalline structure, and be aware of the forces of organisation within its form, a whole world of creative intelligence being expressed in the patterns of matter, the Ring-Pass-Not of the spiritually originated universe.

And then at Christmas, or New Year, be aware that there is also an alternative way out of the cycle, to become a spiral, looking in toward the centre, where is the divine and creative centre, that was in the beginning, still is there now throughout all of what we call time, and shall be the summation of all that ever was. Including us. Here a sufficient image can be the Star of Bethlehem, or the Divine Child it heralds.

Patterns of Community

Most human communities begin as a meeting place of ways. At a crossroads, or often, as in the case of many of our major cities, where there is a crossing of river and of road. Two different elements, land and water, meeting at a point where it is possible for human beings to meet and to trade. Thus the actual site of a community is determined by the natural lie of the land, the configuration of the Earth itself. Human activity then shapes itself around the lineaments of Mother Earth.

From the crossway, a vortex springs up. A vortex of trade and human interchange. Soon a stockade or wall is thrown up to mark its boundaries, its "ring-pass-not" or sacred circle, to protect the little human cosmos that lies within its bounds. Within that circle, surrounding a cross, there springs up a system of fair trading and local law which binds those who dwell within.

And eventually towers begin to rise, set above places of worship, to show that man's true origin, and that of the city, lies in another dimension, signified by their pointing to the heavens. In river, road, bridge, wall, tower and spire, we see the first principles of cosmic expression being re-expressed on Earth in the little works of man.

Thus is the city a focus, a chakrum, a psychic and spiritual centre, a whirling vortex of force within the etheric body of the planet. Capital cities especially form a focus for each nation, even down to the smallest village, for each has a part to play, like minor nadis or lesser chakras within the human body.

As such, towns and cities, and the links between them, are as important in their way as the network of inner energies between mountains, lakes and rivers; or between sacred sites, be they marked by cathedrals or stone circles. Each represents a special type of energy, or mode of interchange. All are different aspects of an inner web upon which they form like crystals of shining dew.

It behoves us then to be aware of this great network, even when we are in the unlikely and uncongenial environs of a smoky and noisy city. To be aware of its local history, its reason for being, and its contribution to the sum total of the soul of the nation. And ultimately to the complete body of humanity as a whole, that is inextricably united with the body of the beloved planet we all share.

The Shadow Side of Spirituality
The shadow side of spirituality reminds me of the more strident type of advertising slogan for various types of detergent: "Whiter than whitest white!" "Adds brightness to perfect whiteness!"

That's all very well as a spiritual aspiration as long as it does not mean looking down upon those who can only aspire to the lighter shades of grey. "Someone's mother isn't using .... yet!" In the esoteric context of this parable, fill in the blank with the name of your latest guru.

This kind of obsession with slogans for branded goods is bad enough when it is only a matter of esoteric fashion. What is the spiritual flavour of the month? Blavatsky? Besant and Leadbeater? Alice Bailey? Krishnamurti? Rudolf Steiner? Edgar Cayce? The Dalai Lama?

Of course in more general terms you can't go far wrong by sticking with the brand name "Aquarian." I can remember in the days of my youth when anyone over the age of forty was looked down upon with ill-disguised pity as being only a poor benighted Piscean. Or at the very best "a person of the Cusp" – only half baked Aquarian.

All this of course is simply the silly fantasising of esoteric adolescence. Although it is surprising how far some people can be taken for a pseudo-spiritual ride. This can develop a more serious aspect when it is compounded with theories of spiritual evolution. Was there not a recent case where a wealthy seeker after truth was rendered considerably less wealthy by being privately assured that he was a rare soul, and had been in a previous incarnation Joseph of Arimathea, no less? In this incarnation all he needed to do to manifest his true spirituality was to make some donations to the worthy cause of his "all-but-ascended-out-of-this-world" initiators. Who did they reckon to be in their previous incarnations one wonders?

Of course most of us are in the fortunate position of not being wealthy enough for anyone to want to bamboozle us in this way. And anyway we would not be taken in with elaborate holograms of the Holy Grail and a subtle line in esoteric confidence trickery, would we?

Funny though, how we move in rather more humdrum circumstances. Despite our inherent spiritual qualities we are not appreciated for what we are. Perhaps there has been a mistake in the recording angel's department as to the true state of our karmic balance sheet. Anyway, until the oversight has been sorted out, if we can't keep up with our dreadful neighbours at least we can esoterically "transcend" them. We wouldn't insist upon it for a moment of course, but we are, we are, if only they did but know it – spiritually more evolved. Not that they would understand what that means, poor dears.

Yet spiritual pride can move from petty to serious if it gets to the stage when we can only speak in hushed confidentiality with a few kindred souls of like evolutionary stature to ourselves. Mutual self-admiration societies may seem harmless if rather sad institutions until human folly begins to take on truly cosmic proportions, as has been recently witnessed when some highly spiritual folk, at any rate by their own evaluation, ended up sticking plastic bags over their heads and going off on a one-way ticket to comet Hale-Bopp.

A Knight of the Drawn Sword

In his book *King Arthur, King of Kings*, Jean Markale, Professor of Celtic History at the Sorbonne in Paris, makes two statements about King Arthur that are worth dwelling upon.

One is that he was "an embodiment of all the hopes of his fellow countrymen." The other that "Arthur's greatness is directly dependent on others' need for him."

At times whenever the group soul of a nation is seeking regeneration, even transformation, then the figure of Arthur can be a focus of inspiration and active change.

As a means to achieve this the *Morte d'Arthur* of Tennyson can be a valuable and evocative meditational tool. Tennyson studied the Arthurian legends very deeply over many years, and his poetic gift allowed him to touch deep levels of national consciousness. Added to this, his clear narrative style and vivid imagery make his work an excellent vehicle for group or personal pictorial meditation.

Reading the poem aloud by candle light or fire light to a group of friends or kindred spirits can evoke the way the original Arthurian tales developed, which was by a bard or travelling conteur weaving stories for the imagination of the encircled court to feed upon.

Try reading the *Morte d'Arthur* then, in this fashion. It tells of the wounded king being carried to the shore of the lake after the last great battle, where he instructs the last surviving knight, the faithful Sir Bedivere, to take his mighty, magical sword Excalibur and cast it into the waters.

Twice Sir Bedivere hesitates to do so, through the kind of plausible motives by which most of us indulge in self-deception and avoidance of spiritual duties. At the third bidding of the king, he does so, and an arm rises from the lake, catches the sword and brandishes it, before disappearing below the waters.

This is the sign for a strange barque, with the mourning queens, to appear, to take the king, before he dies, to the mysterious land of Avalon, where he can be healed of his grievous wounds and await to come again when his people need him. For the lake and mysterious island within it are not physical locations, although certain physical locations may have come to represent them, as an aid to many, but rather are they representative of inner states, of hidden realities, the group unconscious, or the astral plane.

Visualise then, with Tennyson's poetry, the king being carried aboard the mystic boat that takes him to these regions and take to heart his last injunction to Bedivere, who represents within himself as sole survivor, the whole of the Fellowship of the Round Table.

That injunction is that we pray for the king.

Do this then yourself. For by so doing a link will be made between your highest conception of spiritual aspiration – the direct approach to God – and your deep natural heritage as an embodied soul who feels love and reverence for the king.

Then ask within your heart that the king return to guide and protect the nation, together with his queen, and the magician Merlin, and all the knights and ladies, and the Lady of the Lake and the faery women too. You may, if you are sensitive, become aware of some of them, in their redeemed form, having achieved regeneration and transformation on the Isle of Avalon – which is the Earthly Paradise – the pristine Garden of Eden condition.

Finally, be aware of an altar, perhaps of a great cathedral or abbey, or perhaps a more humble one dear to your heart, all are equally holy, and see upon it a great drawn sword – the mighty Excalibur. This is a token that the forces of the once and future king are abroad in the land again, and for your help in this work you may justly regard yourself as a member of a current order – a Knight of the Drawn Sword.

The Other Side of the Door

The last of C.S.Lewis' Chronicles of Narnia, *The Last Battle*, is a book about last things. That is, about death, but also about what follows it, or new beginnings.

Death is represented by a doorway, but much depends upon our faith and belief as we approach and go through that doorway. Our general mental attitude considerably affects our immediate after-death condition.

To those who approach it aright, the other side of death's door brings the possibility of infinite freedom. But the sceptical dwarfs are unable to take advantage of this because of their unbelief, their reluctance to be "taken in." The phrase has a profound and pathetic double meaning.

Immediately on the other side of death's door there is a grove of trees upon which grow the most delicious fruit. It is an apple grove, like Avalon of the legends; and for those who come to this Earthly Paradise, no longer is there any "forbidden fruit" – all is perfect freedom.

To the dwarfs however, stunted in spirit as well as in body, the door they have passed through is still, they are convinced, only the entrance into a dark barn. They sit round in a circle in introverted inability to see the light of the paradisal tree. Even Aslan, their God, cannot help them, for any attempt at communication is misinterpreted by them.

They mistake gentle warnings for threats. They degrade gifts to the level of their own expectations. As Aslan says to the children: "You see, they will not let us help them. They have chosen cunning instead of belief. Their prison is only in their own minds, yet they are in that prison, and so afraid of being 'taken in' that they cannot be taken out."

The end of the book and of the Narnian Chronicles takes place at the end of Narnian time, and all who now face the apparent end of the world come face to face with its creator. There is a choice, dependent on their own free will, even at the last. Those who respond to their creator with love and joy go off to one side of him, to be led to higher things, while those who respond with hate or fear go to the other side, disappearing into his shadow. A concept that might well have come straight from the Rosicrucian mystic Jacob Boehme, whom Lewis was reading at the time of his conversion many years before.

In things pertaining to the high heavens we are dealing with uncreate realities which by their very nature must be incomprehensible to us. Experience of the real heavens can only be expressed in terms of high poetic symbolism. Lewis, writing for children, endeavours to take our imagination "further up and further in" to the divine counterpart of the created Narnia, in a perfect land where all the inner kingdoms are combined, spurs jutting out from the great mountains of God Himself

And so the Chronicles of Narnia end on a high mystic note, concluding with the heaven based statement that all the previous adventures in Narnia were but the first chapter in a greater, heavenly story, that will go on for ever, and in which every chapter will be more glorious than the last.

Bearing the Burden of the Shadow

There is a character in one of the novels of Charles Williams, *Descent into Hell*, who spends most of her life afraid of her shadow side. This takes the form of being afraid that when she is out one day, she will meet her double, coming down the street to meet her. So strong does this fear become that she is almost afraid to venture out of the house alone.

She is enabled to overcome it in the end, however, by instruction in the principle of "substitution", or the Doctrine of Substituted Love, to give it its full name. The spiritual adviser who comes to her aid tells her that whenever she is alone, and thinks she is going to be afraid, she is to put him in her place and let him be afraid instead. He insists that this will be very easy for both of them, and needs only the faith and will to act. He quotes St. Paul as his authority, that we ought "to bear one another's burdens."

He goes on to explain that this means more than mere sympathetic listening, although this may be a helpful part of the process. It is a deliberate agreement and intention for one person to carry the other's burden – just as one might a parcel! This means a handing over by one, and a taking on by the other, in a simple act of agreement.

Williams saw this as a fact of nature, for as his hero says in the novel, after quoting Christ and St. Paul, "anyhow there's no need to introduce Christ, unless you wish. It's a fact of experience. If you give weight to me, you can't be carrying it yourself; all I'm asking you to do is to notice the blazing truth."

Later the process of substitution is described. The character Stanhope (a dramatic poet like Williams) takes on Pauline's conflict of spirit. He does so by visualising the situation that she is frightened of and opening himself to the negative emotions that she might feel as a consequence. He experiences them himself, but because he is not embroiled within the situation by weight of past emotional connotations, it is an altogether lighter burden for him to bear.

Despite its "blazing truth" Williams makes no attempt to explain it. He simply says that "the substitution there, if indeed there is substitution, is hidden in the central mystery of Christendom which Christendom itself has never understood, nor can." One is reminded of Lady Julian of Norwich's immense faithful optimism combined with a refusal to probe into that which is beyond human understanding.

In the end however, Pauline is enabled not only to have her own burden lifted in this manner, but to lift the burdens of others – and this through space and time! She comes, by this means, to the aid of an ancestor who had been condemned to be burned at the stake.

Another major spiritual realisation she comes to is that the "shadow" side of herself that she has been fearful of is in fact not to be feared at all. It turns out to be no horror, but her ideal spiritual self. When the two Paulines are able to meet, the fallen shadow self of her everyday personality, and her unfallen self as originally conceived in heaven, then the true work of her destiny can commence.

The Spiritual Director

Who or what is a Spiritual Director? It is commonly used to signify a particular function in a contemplative order – although it need not be restricted to this specialised context, whereby visions are related to another person to assess their validity. This may be part of the function of a confessor.

In this regard it is not unknown for the Spiritual Director to be somewhat out of his depth and to privately consider that some of his spiritual charges must be mad! Picture the poor unimaginative priest deputed to go and hear the confessions at a local convent if he has to contend with reported angelic or divine visions.

However, that is not our problem, although it does have its parallels in the context of the personal spiritual quest. We can all of us be in either situation. Either of the conscripted "spiritual director" being called upon the assess the worth and validity of someone else's inner experience, or else having had such experiences or visions or realisations ourselves, looking for someone to tell them to. And when and if we do tell, are we expecting to be received with criticism or with credulity?

It seems to me that in spiritual things, as in other areas of life, the proof of the pudding is in the eating. Suppose we look at a parallel situation. If we should be budding poets, or painters, should we seek an artistic director?

It is of course a free country. In the artistic context we are perfectly free to scribble and daub away to our heart's content without seeking any tuition or direction whatsoever. It may be that we are natural geniuses and need no help in our urge to artistic self expression. However, such are likely to be extremely rare.

Most of us will therefore need to find some kind of tuition and critical direction. Where can we find it? In some kind of school, perhaps evening classes, or by enrolling with a personal teacher. Suppose we do not like the attitude of our teacher? We can always change. If we find that we go through a lot in rapid succession without finding the sympathy or appreciation that we feel is due to us, the fault may well be in ourselves.

We can, as an alternative, enlist the sympathy of relatives or friends. Then much depends upon how honest they are with us, or indeed how qualified they are to be honest in the first instance. One is hardly likely to learn colour sense from the colour blind, for example.

If we are really convinced of the worth of our own genius, that is not reflected in the respect of others, we may go to the expensive lengths of publishing our own work or hiring a gallery to get hung. Neither way is to be recommended save as an expensive way of advertising our personal vanity.

So let us look at the same situation in relation to spiritual insights and visions. We can try to find some help and guidance in specific groups or with specific teachers. These are likely to provide reasonable guidance. We can, alternatively, try our relations or our friends. For the most part, unless we are very fortunate, they are not likely to be too helpful. The spiritually colour blind are infinitely more numerous than the physical kind.

If we really feel that we have great revelations to be made we shall have to take steps to see how many people want to attend to us, either in writing articles or on public platforms. This is quite an effective indicator, as in the artistic analogy. How many people are prepared to cross the street, to pay a small admission fee, to listen to us? If not many, then we should beware going to the vanity publisher with our spiritual or philosophical revelations. Our rewards are likely to be as slim as the self-financing novelist, poet or painter. It is a pretty basic universal law that requires us to measure our worth in terms of how well we can communicate meaningfully with other members of the human race.

Of course, the answer to all this does not lie in numbers. As may be seen from the popular press, millions are very willing to subscribe to garbage. And in many years of writing and lecturing I must say the best indicators of success have not been in the applause of large audiences or the number of copies of any particular volume sold, but in the occasional word of thanks from some stranger that something one had said was of real help at some particular time. And in the last analysis this is the only valid spiritual direction.

The right direction for us to be going is in being of some service to others. Often we do not know what that really should be. But if we follow the still small voice within, which is our own true spiritual director, some day and in some way some friend or stranger will thank us. In that instant we will then know that our small inner voice has met with an answering confirmation in the outer world.

Most of the quest for spiritual enlightenment is being able to differentiate between the still small voice and the louder urges of the legion of desires that make up our being. Although some general guidance is possible, by direction or example, from others, in the end we have to make that differentiation ourselves. As I have said, external life will indicate, in time, whether we have chosen aright. And whatever outer spiritual directors we care to choose on our journey, in the end it is the inner spiritual director that is the one we have to choose, from a variety of inner contending voices. And it is not the loudest, nor the one with the greatest external support, that is likely to be right.

Preparation for the Great Transition
If we are going to seek guidance upon physical death and its after effects, it seems best to ask someone from the other side with some experience of it. Not that all such "channelling" is what it claims to be. However, it is the quality of what is said that is important and we must each judge that for ourselves. So without further claims, this is the latest intelligence I have received from a source which seems to me to be authoritative:

"The condition of the newly departed from the outer terrestrial life is a very personal matter. Dying to the world, departing from the imperatives of the flesh, and all the astro-mental moulding that has gone with it, is in a sense an ultimate psychoanalysis or psychotherapy. Your etheric/physical body is to some extent like a jelly mould, fashioned in part by heredity, by upbringing and environment, and the climate of the times. It may often resonate too with experiences of another life, here or in other spheres, or with a lesson to be learned, a spiritual task to be done. And the soul conforms to this mould, even for some time after it is broken.

Although in another sense this image of a gel set within a crystalline mould is not entirely accurate. You might also think in terms of a plant that is grown in a fibre pot, in which the roots at first found sustenance, but then constriction, to the point where they are growing closely bound within themselves, inside, into and through the pot. This is frequently the condition of old age, or of aging, when the soul has outgrown its vehicle and is ready for death.

Not that the soul is always immediately in a state of mind to break the mould. Indeed this may prove to be a gentle and gradual process, wherein the being dreams of life that is past in a kind of idealised way. This is the kind of after-world evidence you find in the testimony of certain spirits of the newly dead, in what have been called the summer-worlds of the spiritualists. Although the tradition is not confined to them for it is a popular conception of ancient or modern pagan heavens, from the happy hunting grounds of the Amerindians to the Valhalla of the Vikings.

This however, is not eternity, simply a passing stage, a place of transition, while the soul recovers its real being, its centre of gravity, to slough off much of the accumulated outer baggage or burdens. What you can usefully do in life is to make a start on this dissolution process. And the most healthful and helpful manner possible is to review your past life as you go, presenting it as an offering, be it good or bad to your transitory eyes, to the all forgiving, all empowering, fount of your creation. By these means, when your turn comes to die, you may find the dissolution process, not, as sometimes occurs, the painful cracking of a rigid mould, or the over long confinement in constricting conditions of delusion or self-indulgent dream, which by their very nature are transitory, for every fantasy must return to reality in the end.

Then the imagination ceases to be bound in the mould into which it was induced by the circumstances, habits of mind and thought patterns of the past life. The patterns of that life are now rather like a sloughed off snake skin. But the memories of earth life continue to exist as part of the capability of the spiritual being. They are of the nature of what we have called 'tracks in space,' which is the nature of a type of memory. Another way of describing it is in the form of an imprint or impression upon the potentiality of the spirit, so that when it desires to manifest in a higher type of world, or spiritual condition far removed from earthly incarnation, it can do so by means of revivifying these images of past lives upon the levels of form. It is like a bank of experiences, that can be drawn upon in appropriate circumstances.

Such circumstances are difficult to describe in terms meaningful to your levels of conception in current earthly terms, but something of the truth is contained in the long sustained belief of the Christian world of the resurrection of the dead. Thus the personality has the potentiality of life within the highest heaven, the paradisal worlds, as they may be remotely conceived by you. But in this condition, washed clean of their imperfections, a process that is depicted in ancient myth by the washer of clothes by the ford, or by Moses instructing the tribes of Israel at Mount Zion to wash their clothes, or by the Christian rite of baptism.

This washing, this cleansing process, is a preparing of your heavenly raiment, which as we have said above, can be commenced in earthly life even as you wear it. What is not done now, as you go, will have to be done later, and indeed can be more effectively performed now. As in worldly washing, stains are easier to remove when they are new.

It is often recommended to esoteric students, and those who seek to prepare themselves for service, to perform an evening review. A time when the events of the day are unrolled before the mind's eye, the inner vision. It is frequently taught that this unrolling of the carpet of experience in space and time should be run backwards. This can be helpful in a psychological manner, it helps to break up conglomerates of action or of thought by reversal of perspective. What however is more important is the tone or manner in which you perform this exercise. It can thus be helpful to visualise yourself kneeling in a chapel of redemption, in the company of other souls, of every age and clime. Concern yourself not with the detail of others who are there, but be aware that you are not alone. Part of a company far removed from you perhaps in temperament or in time but with whom you are united in the common cause of your redemptive purpose here. This awareness of others is a natural remedy against spiritual exclusiveness, and you may also be aware of angelic presences, discerned simply as delicate shapes in the light above the heads of those who are assembled there, the Holy Guardian Angels and their helpers.

Our main concern is that of ourselves and our own account before our Maker. Let the events of your life roll before you, not unduly condemning yourself, or passing judgment, which is as often as not simply an intellectual interference. There is only one judge, one judgement that is here, and that is the sacred heart of the figure that stands before you in light over the altar. Whose presence upon earth is encapsulated in the bread and wine of the sacred host, the sacrament.

I recommend, therefore, that you come here each day. Each evening perhaps when you lie down to rest. And let the experience do the teaching."

Poetry and the Spiritual Dimension

One of the most popular poets in modern times, whose books sold in hundreds of thousands to our parents and grandparents, is hardly ever read nowadays. Most of his books are out of print, and if this is a culturally depressing situation, at least for the discerning, it means that his books can be purchased at bargain prices in secondhand bookshops.

The poet in question is Alfred Noyes (1880-1958) and his poem *The Highwayman* is probably the most anthologised narrative poem in English literature. There can be few, over a certain age, who have not thrilled at some time in their life to the romantic tale of the highwayman and Bess, the inn-keeper's black eyed daughter, who gave her life for him, in the poem of galloping rhythm that starts:

> *The wind was a torrent of darkness among the gusty trees,*
> *The moon was a ghostly galleon tossed upon cloudy seas,*
> *The road was a ribbon of moonlight over the purple moor,*
> *And the highwayman came riding –*
>   *Riding – riding –*
> *The highwayman came riding, up to the old inn-door.*

But Noyes was more than a one poem man. In the years immediately prior to the 1st World War, he raised the spirits of the nation with an epic poem on Sir Francis Drake, and a series of vignettes, *Tales of the Mermaid Tavern*, where the spirit of the Elizabethan period is evoked.

Yet Noyes has fallen out of fashion. So much so that he is no longer even granted a mention in literary reference books, whilst many modern students of English literature have never heard of him. One respected academic text, *A History of Modern Poetry* by Professor David Perkins, expresses the modern attitude that gives the reasons why.

> "Like most poets of his day, he celebrated English landscape, history, and character, which he conceived only in literary conventions. He has an elvish England of twilight witchery, turnstiles, and cottages; a merry England of bowls, beer, roasting crabs, and good Queen Bess; and an eighteenth-century England of country roads and inns, highwaymen and red coats. *Drake*, his blank-verse epic in twelve books, follows the adventures of a sea going hero up to the Armada, and sees in Drake and in England embodiments of political and spiritual freedom. His patriotism is almost embarrassingly simple-minded and fervent, as may be seen also in his *Tales of the Mermaid Tavern*, which deals with the same period of history."

Whilst not wishing to diminish the importance of the main trends of modern poetry with its exploration of individual angst and agonising over lost spiritual directions, we would submit that there remains an important place for poetry of the old school, which sought to encourage and inspire, in patterned rhythmic verse.

Pride in one's national heritage is not necessarily nostalgic sentimentality. Nor is a celebration of the dignity and achievements of the human spirit necessarily a soft centred religiosity, as Professor Perkins implies in his further remark "Noyes also wrote philosophical poems of an uplifting tendency, expressing his conviction that human life and history are related to a Divine Being and purpose."

What he is referring to is Noyes' later work, a celebration of the human spirit of intellectual and scientific enquiry, under the title of *The Torch-Bearers*, a series of evocations of the men who looked to the stars, (Copernicus, Tycho Brahe, Galileo, Newton and William and Sir John Herschel) and of those who looked to the wisdom in the Earth (from Pythagoras and Aristotle through to Goethe and Darwin) and finally a celebration of the now much taken for granted ability for worldwide human communication by radio.

But whilst admittedly Noyes' verse had its occasional defects (he wrote much and rapidly, spurred on by early success, and so later revised some of his early work) his total ostracism seems an over reaction by modern sentiment that implies that the fault lies largely in the eye of the beholder, rather than in Noyes' shortcomings.

What is of interest to anyone who is prepared to share Noyes' academically derided "conviction that human life and history are related to a Divine Being and purpose" lies in some of the roots of his poetic inspiration. As a young boy he was brought up in west Wales. An imaginative child with a natural literary bent, he would spend many hours in the woods overlooking the sea near his home. In a clearing on the cliff face overlooking the tops of the pine trees below, he spent many enchanted hours feeding his imagination, not only on the natural sights and sounds but on the images within the books that he had brought with him, including Spenser's *Faerie Queen*. What did a nine-year-old boy find in the works of an Elizabethan courtier written nearly 300 years before? As he later recalled, although he never intellectually unravelled the intricacies of the story, it was for him "a ramble through a wild country of enchantment."

But beyond the images of his reading, which included Keats, Wordsworth and Sir Walter Scott, there came into his mind the presence of another. A being not seen by any but the young boy, a strange fey creature who seemed to slip into his awareness like the dappled shadows of leaves upon the page of an open book. And so the name that he gave to this faery visitant was naturally "Shadow-of-a-Leaf."

There are of course many children who have imaginary companions, most of whom fade with approaching adulthood, but in Alfred Noyes' case Shadow-of-a-Leaf never left him, and he later described him as "an invisible friend ... a kind of Ariel who could open doors into unseen worlds." He even appears in various forms in Noyes' work over the years: as a kind of elfin figure in some of his lyric poetry; in the guise of the Fool of Maid Marian in his play *Sherwood*; and in *The Torch-Bearers* almost as an earth-angel of tremendous power emerging from the depths of the Grand Canyon who then leads the poet in a series of visions through time.

Shadow-of-a-Leaf could also inspire metrical innovations in Noyes' poetry, as in the sequence of Mary Queen of Scots in *Tales of the Mermaid Tavern*. It was, in a way, the influence of Shadow-of-a-Leaf, a creature intimately associated with trees, who helped Alfred Noyes to write his most famous and much loved poem *The Highwayman*, for the first line came into his head one blustery night from the sound of the wind through the trees on Bagshot Heath, Sussex, in those days (1904) still quite wild country. It took him about two days to complete the poem and it appeared shortly afterwards in *Blackwood's Magazine*.

W.B.Yeats was sufficiently impressed with the magical quality of some of Alfred Noyes' early lyric poetry that he sought to arrange for one of his poems to be chanted to the accompaniment of a psaltery at one of his programmes of Celtic renaissance at the Abbey Theatre, Dublin. Sir Herbert Beerbohm-Tree, the great Edwardian actor and theatrical impresario sought to stage a dramatised version of Noyes' faery narrative poem *The Forest of Wild Thyme* (in an attempt to make up for his mistake in rejecting Barrie's *Peter Pan*!) However, the outbreak of war put paid to this proposal.

Some twenty years later the vividness of the poet's evocation of early astronomers in *The Torch-Bearers* caused the scientist and spiritualist Sir Oliver Lodge to hypothesise, if not assume, that the spirits of the great astronomers might have been in contact with Noyes, either clairvoyantly or subconsciously. However, his attempts to interest Noyes in spiritualism met with little sympathy. Noyes, who had anyway found a spiritual home in the Roman Catholic church, never felt quite satisfied with the provenance of the films or plates from which the pictures of "some rather ghastly apparitions" had been developed.

Yet Sir Oliver might not have been so far wrong. From the evidence of his writing, Noyes seems to have been a natural intuitive and mystic by no means insensitive to psychic impressions. And although some of his verse may not have weathered well with time, like his contemporary narrative poets, Masefield, Chesterton, Kipling, there is a core of spiritual integrity and inspiration in his work that can serve as a welcome and much needed antidote to the trend of much modern poetry, which has tended to become ever more personal, subjective, riddled with anxiety and disillusioned with the state of the human soul. Qualities that suggest sickness – a canker within the rose of the spirit – rather than health.

These old purveyors of story lit a torch that shines across the years, and it will be much to our loss, if, through our indifference, we let it go.

From various issues of "Open Centres" magazine, 1988-98.

6

the importance of coleridge

THE POET Samuel Taylor Coleridge might be considered probably the most authoritative of modern writers on the ancient Mystery tradition. Although born in 1772 he deserves to be considered a modern writer in view of the fact that he was far ahead of his time. He was barely understood by his contemporaries, and only in the 20th century has the significance of his thought become increasingly apparent. He approached the traditional wisdom not only with intuitive understanding but with the intellectual equipment of being able to read the classic texts in their original languages.

Charles Lamb, who was at school with him, records this precocious erudition as follows: "How have I seen the casual passer through the cloisters stand still, entranced with admiration (while he weighed the disproportion between the speech and the garb of the young Mirandula), to hear thee unfold, in thy deep and sweet intonations, the mysteries of Iamblichus, or Plotinus (for even in those years thou waxedst not pale at such philosophical draughts) or reciting Homer in his Greek, or Pindar..." He also read Plato at school and, whilst at Cambridge, the works of Jacob Boehme.

In 1795, at the age of 23, he met and struck up close acquaintance with William Wordsworth, which culminated in the *annus mirabilis* of 1798 when his best poetry was written, and *Lyrical Ballads* by Wordsworth and Coleridge was first published. This was also the culmination of a theory of the creative powers of the mind that they had been formulating, which we shall shortly examine.

They shortly afterwards visited Germany where Coleridge studied deeply the contemporary German romantic philosophy of which Hegel and Schelling were principal exponents.

Sublimely equipped intellectually and creatively to produce a philosophical system that could counteract the distressing split between the subjective and material worlds that had dominated (and still does) the intellectual assumptions of the western world, regrettably he fell far short of his potential.

The main cause of this was an addiction to opium, contracted originally by liberal doses of laudanum to quell the pains of ill health. It may have had a certain advantage in loosening some of the girders of the mind to enable him to become an astute psychologist far ahead of his time, but it also produced a lassitude and lack of concentration that made any large and systematic work impossible.

We are therefore faced with a daunting ill-sorted mass of note books, marginalia, anecdotes of friends and acquaintances, and some patchy prose works and poetry in which brilliant insights flash like gems in a junk shop — though nothing that Coleridge wrote is ever junk. It may often appear irrelevant to the topic in hand, or prone to be borrowed from an author in some other language, but there is a coherent system of thought behind it for those with the application and discernment to discover it.

Fortunately much of the work has been done for us by professional scholars, although some intellectual assumptions by academic workers in the "Coleridge industry" reveal little but their own shortsightedness. It needs a wide clear vision to appreciate the vast mind of Coleridge, which does not always go with academic erudition.

Perhaps the best survey is not written by a professional literary critic at all but by the remarkably learned country solicitor, and follower of Rudolf Steiner, Owen Barfield, who has subsequently become a visiting lecturer to some American university campuses. Even his book, *What Coleridge Thought*, published by the Wesleyan University Press, Middleton, Connecticut, is not an easy read. This is not because he is an obscure author, it is because the assumptions necessary to understand Coleridge's thought are radically at variance with the 17th century Cartesian assumptions that have been embraced by modern western thought, and which now, by customary usage, even appear to be "common sense." In fact these Cartesian assumptions are no more than a fashion in thinking, and an aberrated fashion at that.

Fortunately for students of the esoteric wisdom Coleridge's concepts will not appear so strange. Their particular importance is that they give an occult system of philosophy that is worked out from first principles, without recourse to previous superstitions of the medieval and renaissance periods (with which all thought of the time was tainted) nor influenced by the influx of Eastern concepts (and misunderstanding of Eastern concepts) that swept into the West in the late 19th century as a result of the spiritual/psychic vacuum caused by materialistic intellectualism in church, science and state.

In laying out a scheme of Coleridge's thought we shall therefore have to define our terms carefully, for he used his terms in a sense that is different from common speech on the one hand and from traditional occult (e.g. Qabalistic) terminology on the other.

He sees the human psyche expressing itself through certain faculties which may be listed out as:

REASON
IMAGINATION
UNDERSTANDING
....
UNDERSTANDING
FANCY
SENSE

Reason is the highest faculty of the human being, and is not merely intellect. Mere intellect is called the Understanding by Coleridge. For him the term Reason is what might be more commonly designated in modern esoteric circles as the Spirit.

Understanding, or the power of ratiocination that is present in humans and higher animals, is divided by a bar to designate two modes of it. The lower mode is that which derives from sense experience – and the association of ideas demonstrated in dogs by Pavlov is a limited example of this. The higher mode, found only in humans (so far as we can judge) is ratiocination irradiated by reason, intuitively aware of the higher realms of existence beyond the material.

Imagination and **Fancy** are principally pictorial modes of mind use. Fancy is again a form of simple association of images derived from sense experience. Imagination, on the other hand, is a fusing, transforming, transcending faculty that is creative in its powers of

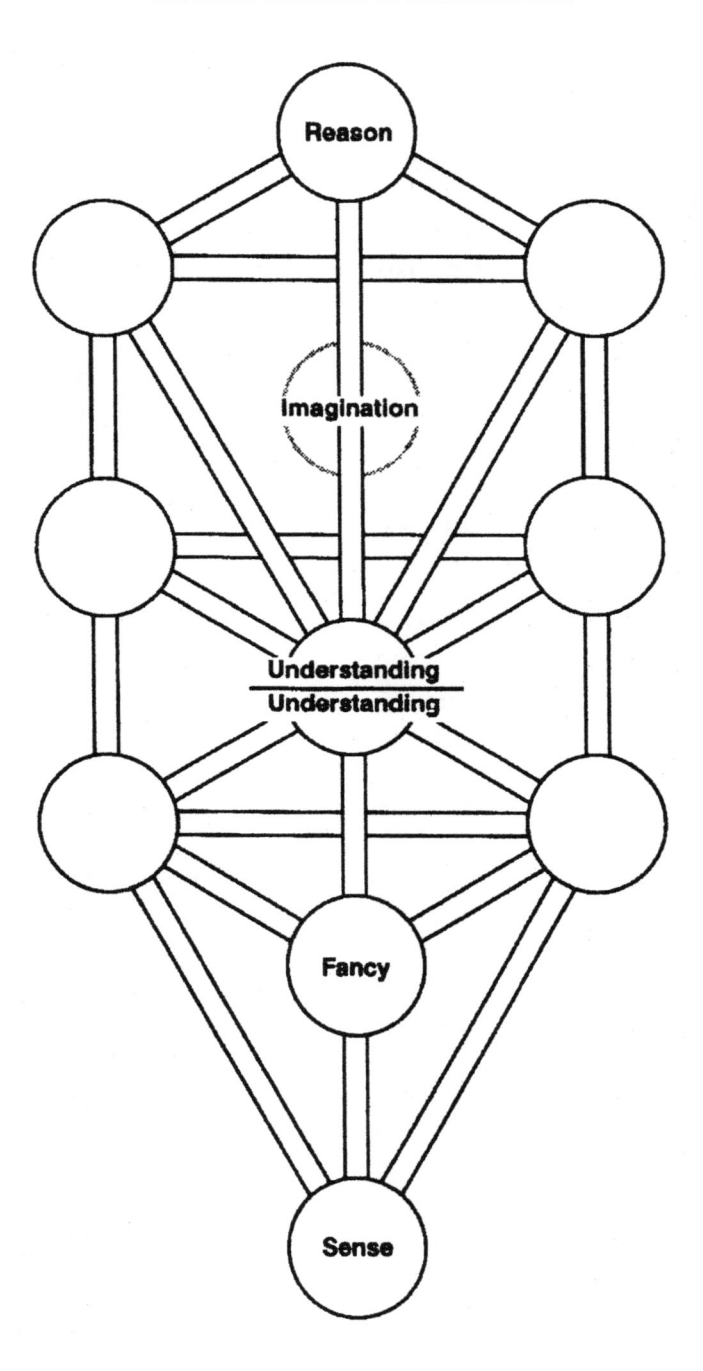

Figure 20: Coleridge's System on the Tree of Life

changing and refining ideas and images. It is a coordinating rather than a mere agglomerative power, and is found in its highest forms of expression in works of art.

It would be possible to align Coleridge's system with the Middle Pillar of the Tree of Life, in which case we would have the diagram in Figure 20.

In this we might recall one of the titles of Yesod as being "the Treasure House of Images;" that is, a teeming sphere of images derived from sensory experience.

At the same time the Coleridgean system throws light on the creative aspect of Daath, the much misunderstood "invisible" Sephirah.

As with the system of the Tree of Life, properly understood, it is important not to regard these categories as separated discretely from one another like the tiers on a wedding cake. They are simply different foci for the expression of the whole consciousness.

There is a sense in which they can be considered as progressively developed in that Life (the evolving Whole of which we all form a part) shows an increasing tendency to individualisation through a process of increasing diversity in unity – that is, a splitting of parts into specialised functions with increased interdependence of the whole upon the organic parts, and of the parts upon the whole organism.

Thus in the mineral stage of life (and by definition, "whatever is, lives") there is uniformity throughout. A piece of pure metal, for instance, is to all intents and purposes of the same character as any other piece of the same substance. There is a movement toward higher organisation however in the crystal, or the magnet.

In plant and animal life we find the increasing development of organs, combining to sustain unitary life, to the point where the principal difference becomes, not physical complexity, but expression of consciousness. And it could be said, in a somewhat crude analogy, that:

minerals are life in a state of dreamless sleep;
plants are dreamers;
animals somnambulists;
the mass of men day-dreamers;
the philosopher, or fully individualised man, fully awake and aware of objective realities.

If we were to apply such a scheme to the Tree of Life, all but the last category would fall below the horizontal bar at Tiphareth.

This bar, which divides the Tree in two, in a fundamental vertical polarity, is of supreme practical importance. Above it is that which is creative; below it is that which is created.

In Nature, Coleridge designated this division by two Latin terms:

NATURA NATURANS   "naturing" nature – or creative nature;

NATURA NATURATA   "natured" nature – or created nature.

This is the complete antithesis of the materialist viewpoint that all consciousness evolved from matter. Rather it considers all matter (i.e. dormant created life and its increasing organisation into higher life forms and thence into dawning higher consciousness) to be projected creations by the denizens of the world of archetypal ideas and spiritual wills.

In more familiar esoteric terminology, as applied to the human being, this represents the Higher Self and Lower Self. It is important to realise its application to all other forms of life though, at whatever stage of evolution. In esoteric tradition this would be accounted for by the various angelic or devic powers considered to be behind nature.

We might make a simple illustration, as in Figure 21, without attempting to be comprehensive of all life forms.

It follows from this that at our higher levels of consciousness we are at one with, or of the same kind, as the forces behind nature. Just as we share the same physical atoms and astral or emotional picture images with all lower created life.

It was to bring about a realisation of this, divorced from any occult overtones (with the all too familiar dubious associations of sensationalism, credulity and power-mongering) that much of Wordsworth's and Coleridge's poetry was written. Even pieces such as Wordsworth's on the daffodils, done to death in school anthologies, are evocations of higher consciousness; and his work is full of similar material. Coleridge's *Rime of the Ancient Mariner* and the unfinished *Cristobel* are more overt metaphysical treatises.

Indeed, it could well be argued that for a course in practical occultism, rather than spend much intellectual effort in categorising the various inner beings from occult textbooks, it

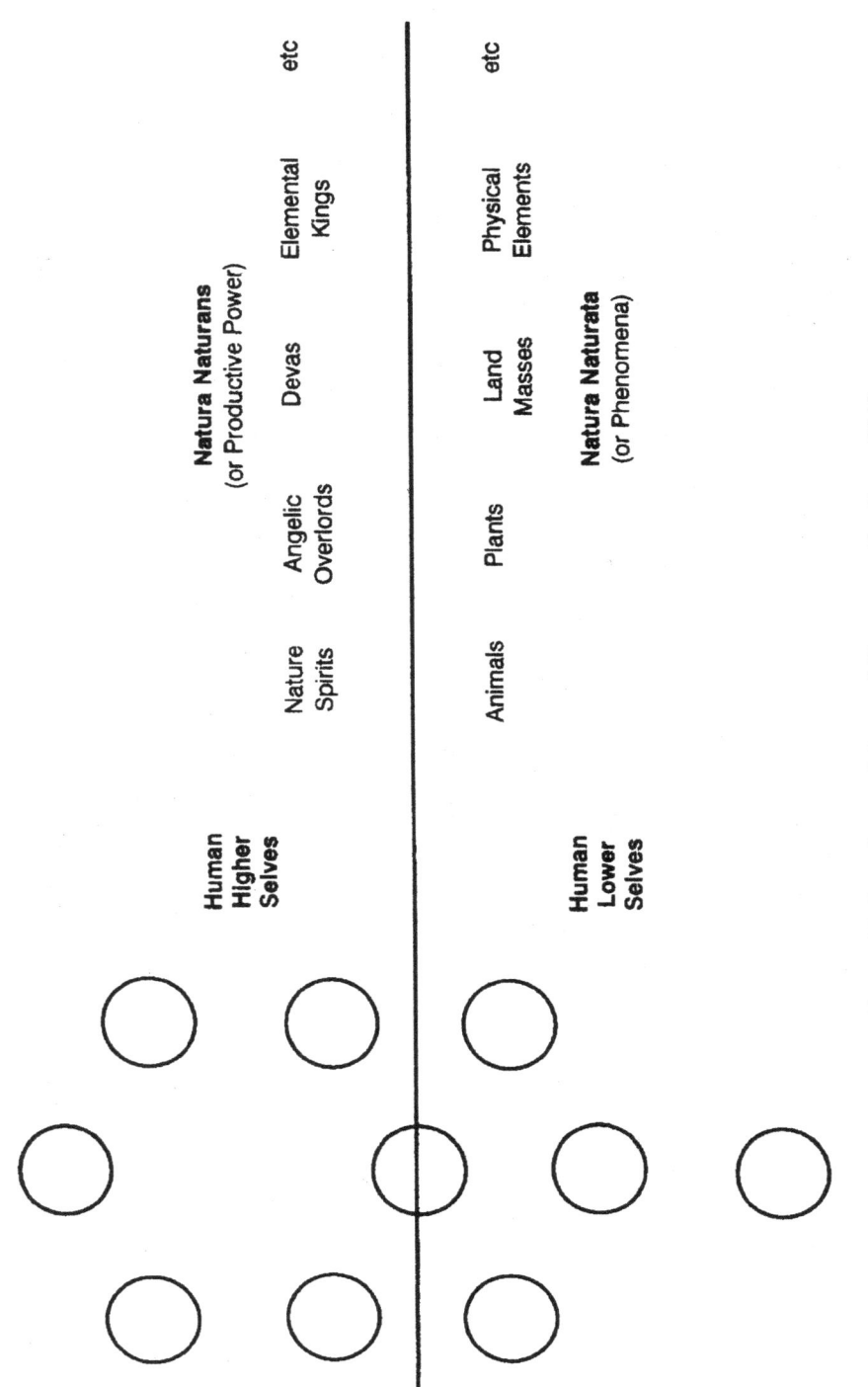

Figure 21: Creating and Created Nature on the Tree of Life

would be far more effective to read contemplatively a few of these poems and then go into the countryside and attempt to experience a similar vision.

The first is for the most part an operation of the lower understanding – the latter is an active attempt at the higher use of the imagination. The former may confer secondhand learning, the latter should give active experience. Magic is where you find it, even in the pages of *Palgrave's Golden Treasury*. So much for occult secrecy!

This leads on, however, to deeper philosophic considerations, concerned with the mechanism of our perception.

We have been conditioned by modern science, and its influence on our education, to regard reality as something behind the visible appearances. That is, for instance, that the colour, texture and hardness of the desk upon which I write are secondary "illusions" of a grey reality behind, of electromagnetic forces directly discernible only through an electron microscope. To Coleridge such an idea would have been utterly false, as we shall try to show.

> All reality is in fact immediate.
>
> We create reality in polar relationship with others.
>
> What we practice is what IS.

We feel it necessary to present these as bare axiomatic statements. They may thus seem arbitrary. But they are no more arbitrary than the assumptions made by Descartes, and followed by materialistic promulgators of "the scientific method" who assume that "the subjective" is separate from "the objective."

They are difficult to grasp and accept because Cartesian dualism, by ingrained habit of thought, has the appearance of being obvious and commonsense. As Blake said, however, we need to cleanse the doors of perception. And the cleansing that has to take place is of our Cartesian assumptions. These we took in at our mother's knee, without necessarily ever have heard of Descartes or reading his philosophy, which the scientific establishment assumes to be the basis of reality (with the possible recent exception of nuclear physics, where the system is beginning to break down under experiment).

A further difficulty is that the Understanding (below the line) is commonly regarded as the ultimate judge of objective reality –

although this prejudice too is beginning to crumble in the light of experience.

The Understanding – unless of the higher kind, irradiated by Reason – can only apprehend phenomena. And it can only attempt to explain phenomena by recourse to another line of phenomena (atoms, molecules, force-fields, etc.) From this, various scientific theories may be spun, but these are but illusory webs of fancy attempting to explain appearances; and although later scientific thought may smile with indulgence on earlier fancies such as the theories of phlogiston, caloric, animal magnetism, geocentrism, catastrophism, or whatever, the current fancies couched in terms of higher mathematics are no nearer to fundamental reality.

For a more detailed examination of this problem the student is recommended to study Owen Barfield's *Saving the Appearances*, published in paperback by Harcourt Brace Inc.

In the words of Coleridge: "The solution of phaenomena can never be derived from phaenomena." We have to grasp the fact that the underlying reality of things is not matter – or any equivalent inanimate base external from ourselves – but is an immaterial relationship.

In other words, a principle of polarity lies at the foundation of the world. This is no news to Qabalists but the practical applications and implications of the two Pillars of the Temple may not have been fully realised in their immediacy.

Generally speaking, the Qabalistic student is content to apply the polar concepts of the Pillars to the world as it is perceived according to current scientific theory. For instance in the positive and negative polarity of electrical or magnetic fields. This has validity to a point, but only as an analogy, or faint reflection, of the fundamental polar principle which by its closeness to our immediate perceptions, we fail to apprehend.

This basic polarity lies, firstly, between the creator and the created; that is, between natura naturans and natura naturata; between human Higher Self and Lower Self; species oversoul and plant or animal species; Elemental King and Elemental concourse of natural features, etc. We might call this, at least for diagrammatic convenience, "vertical polarity."

Equally important however is its "horizontal" application between creators, and between their creations, which produces the worlds of perceived phenomena. In psychological terms this is an act of imagination. Our imagination constructs the world that appears about us.

The act of perception, which is instantaneous and unconscious in its workings, is an activity of what Coleridge called **Primary Imagination.**

Thus do we create ourselves, in conjunction with the related other, the face of the beloved, the man in the Clapham omnibus, the stars in the telescope's lens.

In the fully conscious highly evolved man, these perceptions, or primary imaginative pictures of relationships with others, are presented for assimilation by the higher powers. That is, the powers of higher Understanding (or Understanding irradiated by Reason); secondary or creative Imagination; and pure spiritual Reason.

The lower powers, of Sense, Fancy and lower Understanding – good servants but bad masters – provide functions, of perception, memory and logical deduction respectively – all of which can nowadays be reproduced to a limited extent in computing devices. Human nature in its fullness is, however, capable of rather more than the silicon chip.

It is by Reason and Imagination that we achieve our fullness as human beings. The Understanding, with its powers of analysis based upon experience, is a necessary device whereby we realise our own detachment from a common group, as discrete and individual beings. However, it needs to give way, or to be enlightened, by the Imagination and Reason, which allow us to realise a higher form of unity and attachment, or, in Charles Williams' felicitous expression, "co-inherence."

The realisations of Imagination and Reason are not easily formulated and grasped by the Understanding for, being polar, they tend to be expressible only in terms of paradox, or in terms of symbolic truth, as in parable or myth.

We enter the realm of Ideas, in Plato's sense, of living archetypes: "the prophetic soul of the wide world dreaming on things to come." Plato's nous is very similar in conception to Coleridge's Reason, and also to Francis Bacon's lux intellectus or lumen siccum. Bacon, called by Coleridge the British Plato, has been profoundly misrepresented by shallower advocates of "the scientific method" who claim for him, as for Giordano Bruno and even Sir Isaac Newton, their own metaphysical shallowness.

Plato and Bacon are interesting as approaching the same higher truth from different aspects. Plato is primarily concerned with truth at the ideal pole of metaphysical ideas, whereas Bacon approaches it at the material pole as expressed in nature.

Plato often calls Ideas "living laws." Bacon names laws of nature "Ideas".

The importance of Bacon in the history of ideas is that his works mark a change of direction in human contemplation of truth, not a wilful limitation of science to the lower Understanding and the Senses — the so-called scientific method. This is a later aberration, by lesser men.

Coleridge's Reason, then, is the substance of ultimate reality; the power that produces and sustains the natural world. It is also the source of all laws of nature. In another sense it is God. This raises profound theological as well as psychological, philosophical and scientific questions.

In the human being, Reason (or the Spirit in other terminologies) irradiates consciousness throughout the whole evolutionary cycle. It is present to conscious understanding, however, in one of two different modes.

Although present, it may not be realised as being present, and therefore will be "unconscious", or on the other hand it may be self-consciously realised to be present.

We can tabulate various terms to try to indicate each of these two modes of Reason manifesting in the human psyche:

Conscious Self-Knowledge	Unconscious Self-Knowledge
Positive Reason	Negative Reason
Active Reason	Passive Reason
Reason Awake	Dreaming Reason
Conceptual Reason	Ideal Reason
Lux intellectus	Lumen a luce
Understanding "above the line"	Understanding "below the line"

In its negative mode, unrealised and unconscious, it simply gives individuality to man (in itself, of course, no mean achievement on the evolutionary scale).

In its positive mode, it gives the spiritual awakening of the individual human being, (which is a yet higher level of attainment in the evolution of consciousness.)

From this it will be evident that the distinction between Reason and Understanding is crucial. The unenlightened man, be he however intellectually brilliant or knowledgeable, is one in whom Understanding has completely swallowed Reason. If he persists in remaining dominated by Understanding he is as a dreamer refusing to be awakened – or an intellectual corpse refusing the golden destiny of resurrection.

There is a paradox in the identity and action of Reason. It bestows individuality yet at the same time it can never be considered plural; it is, in essence, one and indivisible. An analogy may help the understanding of this paradox. We might consider all human individuals to be like burning candles – yet the light that individually they maintain is one indivisible principle that can be passed from one to another without diminishing itself.

Thus as well as the two modes of Reason that we have tabulated, there are also aspects of Reason – its individuality and its universality or super-individuality.

Reason bestows individuality to what would otherwise be a group-soul dominated animal psyche, by giving the faculty of abstraction, of generalising, of consequent detachment from sense phenomena and the ability to sort and categorise them in terms of universals; that is, to compare.

This gives rise to logic – the ability to see whether any two conceptions in the mind are, or are not, in contradiction to each other. This faculty also implies a sense of detachment – of himself as an autonomous unit, as subject as object, in distinction from the environment.

However, this exercise of the passive or negative mode of Reason, which gives awareness of the aspect of individuality, is but a prison house if it becomes wholly concerned with the logic of difference in the realm of natura naturata, or created nature.

The paradox is brought about by a fundamental quality of Reason, which is behind all manifest phenomena that consciousness can become aware of. That quality is the principle of Polarity.

We may now perhaps begin to comprehend why, on the Tree of Life, and in Coleridge's scheme, Imagination is placed between

Reason and Understanding. (In Qabalistic terms, why Daath appears between Kether and Tiphareth.)

Linked to Understanding by the creative imagination Reason may make itself known to the human psyche. When it fails to do so then a lower condition prevails whereby Reason is swallowed up by the lower Understanding and the negative reason of logic dominates attempted understanding of natura naturata (Malkuth) through the play of fancy in various theories, hypotheses and mental bric-a-brac of the unenlightened "scientific" mind. This applies even in so-called religious sectors of life when an intellectually dogmatic and spiritually dry theology prevails over direct mystical consciousness, or prophetic intuition.

The language of the Imagination is not the categorising limitations of logical classification (which, of course, does have its legitimate place in the powers of human consciousness – it is the abuse and hubris only that we condemn) but in the enlarging dimensions of symbol and myth.

It would be appropriate therefore to make use of the mythical imaginative faculty to try to present to Understanding what is the nature of Reason. This, as Coleridge himself realised, is aptly portrayed in the myth of Prometheus.

In a lecture delivered in 1825 to the Royal Society of Literature, entitled *The Prometheus of Æschylus*, Coleridge enumerated the following points:

That in the generation of the nous, or pure reason in man:

i) it was super-added or infused, and no mere evolution of the animal basis;

ii) it was "stolen" from heaven, to mark its difference in kind from the qualities common to man and the higher animals;

iii) its source in "heaven" marks its superiority as well as essential diversity;

iv) it was a "spark" to mark that it is subject to no modifying reaction from that upon which it acts; it suffers no change from the inferior but multiplies itself by conversion without being alloyed by or amalgamated with that which it enobles, potentiates and transmutes;

v) it was stolen by a "god", and one of the dynasty before Jove, because Jove was the binder of reluctant powers, the coercer and entrancer of free spirits into the fetters of shape, mass and passive mobility. At the same time Prometheus was a god of the same race and essence as Jove, and linked in earlier days in closest and friendliest intimacy with him, to mark the pre-existence, in order of thought, of the nous, as spiritual, to the later products of the "coagulations of spirit" (to use Leibnitz's terms) and the objects of sense.

In other words, the spark of Reason deriving from a god anterior to the Jovian dynasty (that is, to the submersion of spirits in material forms) marks the nous as timeless, or eternal; superior to and different from all things that subsist in space and time. Indeed superior even to souls and understanding consciousness that, though spaceless, partake in the world of time.

The soul, or understanding, if defined physiologically as the principle of sensitivity and growth expressed through the organs of perception, must be considered as the same in kind, if higher in degree, as the consciousness of animals. The spirit, or nous, is that which distinguishes animals from man.

Coleridge then sums up his interpretation of the myth of Prometheus as being the definition of IDEA and LAW.

We capitalise these two concepts as they are fundamental to an understanding of how Reason may be apprehended.

Coleridge regards them as "correlatives that mutually interpret each the other." As might be expected, Reason expresses itself in terms of polarity — neither pole of which can be fully considered without the other.

Ideas of Reason are the only way that the principle of Reason can be considered to be plural. (In similar vein one might talk of "flames" of "light", or "sparks" of "fire.") And these Ideas of Reason are not to be confused with ideas in the ordinary sense, for which Coleridge tends to use terms such as "notions," "conceptions," or "maxims." The latter are simply the products of the lower Understanding, which is incapable of saying very much about Reason and its Laws and Ideas. For this we have to take recourse to Imagination, in symbolism and myth.

There is an identification between the unity of Reason and the multiplicity of the Ideas of Reason — a multiplicity in unity and a unity in multiplicity that is not readily expressed or comprehended in terms of the intellect or lower understanding. The unity and multiplicity are linked in an all-comprehending mutual polarisation.

If one wanted to express it in mathematical terms it would need to be expressed in the equation 1 = 2, or more accurately 1 = n, where n equals all numbers or any number. Coleridge sometimes used a little shorthand symbol to denote this paradox, similar to the astrological sign of Pisces, meaning "in polarity with."

In practical terms then, it is impossible for the lower Understanding to find or give reasons for the qualities of Reason and the Ideas of Reason. They simply are and have to be accepted as facts of higher experience, in common with most existential realities — birth, death, growth, etc. And by reason of the close polarity, whatever is said about Ideas of Reason may also be said about Reason itself. And anything we can say about either can only be conveyed in terms of symbol, by figurative or poetic language of the Imagination.

We must also divest ourselves of the assumption that, as with any ordinary subjective notion or fancy we are "having an Idea." Rather, the reverse is the case, the Idea is having us!

This correlates with the expressed experience of many poets in saying that when it comes to poetic composition of the highest order then a brooding sense of presence is felt and the poem happens to the poet, who with luck, skill and application, may be able to express it and write it down. This is the mechanics of poetic inspiration, or inspiration in any of the arts or indeed other endeavours of creative thought in man. Inspiration is, of course, a much abused term and requires considerable preparation and hard work at the craft of expression (be it musical, linguistic, scientific or technical) before the personality is likely to be an appropriate vehicle for it — although the rare child prodigy or "primitive" artist may be an exception. The important point is that the Idea happens to the receiver of it and, if accurately expressed, may then happen to others who read the poem, listen to the symphony, study the scientific theory or mathematical proof, or even in chess problem to be greatly moved by its purity and elegance, by its truth and beauty.

This is a most important consideration when we come to study the laws of nature, and the method by which we examine the world about us and strive to comprehend the laws of nature – for they are physically expressed spiritual Ideas.

From what we have so far described, the lower Understanding will be hard put to find any method that will bring about enlightenment as to the fundamental laws of nature.

The "scientific method" is much vaunted by the intellectual establishment of the past three or four hundred years, but is no more fitted to comprehend the higher realities that govern existence than is the computer – the diligent, useful, systematic but fundamentally stupid product and tool of the scientific method.

It is the logical extension of the encyclopaedic cataloguing of the botanist Linnaeus. Impressive though his achievements at classification may have been, it is no more than the arrangement of fragments of natura naturata according to an arrangement projected upon it by memory and fancy. As a method it simply ignores the natura naturans that produces the natura naturata.

The discovery of Laws is an altogether different operation, as the inspired Isaac Newton well knew when he discovered the Law of Gravitation. He simply refused to enter into hypothetical conjectures as to how the Law works. And all attempts to explain the problem of "action at a distance" are but the play of fancy – whether they be relatively crude conceptions such as "invisible string" or "universal ether" or relatively sophisticated such as Einstein's General Theory of Relativity.

The rebuff to the lower Understanding is best appreciated if we revert to the table of the powers of the soul of man and consider its vertical polarities as in Figure 22. There is a close connection between the highest and the lowest terms, between Reason and Sense, as there is between Imagination and Fancy (which can be confused by the less discerning) and between the superficially similar higher and lower aspects of Understanding.

Just as Sense is the level where there is direct perception of physical fact – so is Reason the level where there is direct perception of metaphysical fact. The intermediate levels of consciousness are more subjective – a digestion or rumination upon the direct experience of Sense or Reason.

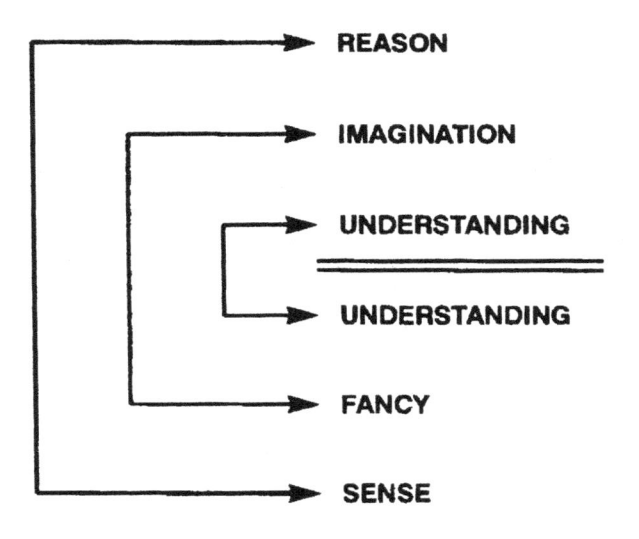

```
┌─────────► REASON
│
│  ┌──────► IMAGINATION
│  │
│  │  ┌───► UNDERSTANDING
│  │  │     ═══════════════
│  │  └───► UNDERSTANDING
│  │
│  └──────► FANCY
│
└─────────► SENSE
```

Figure 22: Interrelationships of Levels of Consciousness

It follows that there is much to be gained from the contemplation of the Ideas of Reason. Far from being impractical abstractions they are a gazing upon a fundamental inner reality upon which all phenomena depends.

Coleridge compares the apprehension of an Idea of Reason with the experience of listening to music; one is at the same time constructing and being constructed by it. He describes them also as "the prophetic soul of the wide world dreaming on things to come." And in his *Treatise on Method* he states that reflection on metaphysical ideas (such as the idea of a perfect circle in geometry) will develop a capacity for "inward beholding", which is our means of access to the Ideas of Reason.

It is true that the mental activity of forming theories and hypotheses may lead the mind to a similar apprehension of Ideas of Reason. Thus in the search for a theory the mind may rise to apprehending a Law, but the fundamental Laws (Platonic Ideas, or "living laws", Bacon's "Ideas") should not be confused with the general run of scientific "laws" that are simply a cataloguing of sense observations according to certain prejudiced assumptions.

The modern scientific spirit would no doubt take exception to being accused of prejudiced assumptions. However, this is because those prejudiced assumptions are so mentally ingrained as axiomatic that they are never regarded as subject to question.

The most glaring assumption upon which all modern science is based (except perhaps in certain areas of advanced atomic physics) is that there is an absolute dichotomy between mind and matter, between subjective and objective, between the observer and the phenomena observed. It is, in fact, no more than a useful fiction promulgated by the 17th century philosopher Descartes which has now outlived its usefulness.

Another assumption that masquerades as proven fact is that of "uniformitarianism", the assumption that the remote past (be it in geology, palaeontology or biology) is only to be interpreted in the light of what can be observed in the present order of nature.

But if Coleridge is right (and he has the support of a number of important thinkers, from Hegel to Goethe) and physical process cannot be divorced from mental processes, nor natural science from human and ethical psychology, then a whole concourse of scientific pictures of the universe may have to be abandoned – from the billions of years of palaeontology to the billions of light years of astronomy. They may prove to be but the flickering illusions of parallel mirrors.

The whole nature of science needs radical examination. It has been a useful tool, and it needed to free itself as a discipline from the tyranny of organised religion, but organised science has now become the new tyrant.

Fortunately the internal contradictions of the scientific method will bring about a change. This is already becoming evident in physics, where experiment is showing that the act of observing is part of the object observed. This has led to a number of books correlating ideas of modern physics with concepts of Eastern mysticism, for instance, *The Tao of Physics*, by Fritjof Capra.

At the same time, in the organic realm, where the young science of ecology is revealing the dire consequences of man's technological rape of the Earth, there are obvious danger signals that somewhere along the line, scientific man has got things all wrong – that ruthless exploitation, be it in terms of vivisection, or driving species to extinction, in terms of polluting nature or laying waste all earth's natural resources, cannot be continued with impunity from dire self-destructive consequences.

There are also religious as well as scientific consequences to consider as an extension of Coleridge's world view. Man may be a spatial object in nature, in common with all the other objects, but when we disregard the Cartesian assumption that subjective and objective are separate categories of existence, then it follows that nature is as much in man as man is in nature. They interpenetrate or co-inhere.

The same principle is at work between man and woman as individual and humankind as a social entity. They cannot in truth be regarded as separate categories of being. The whole of human society is in man just as man is in human society.

And equally there is a similar principle in relation to man and God. God is in man and man is in God. God is therefore also in human society and human society in God. This is another way of looking at Reason, for Coleridge states quite explicitly in his lecture on Prometheus that "God is Reason."

We could, from these considerations, draw up a symbolic figure in Figure 23, on the same lines as ancient attempts to portray the mystery of the Holy Trinity. This is because the natural expression of Three-in-One God will be in and through a triune nature.

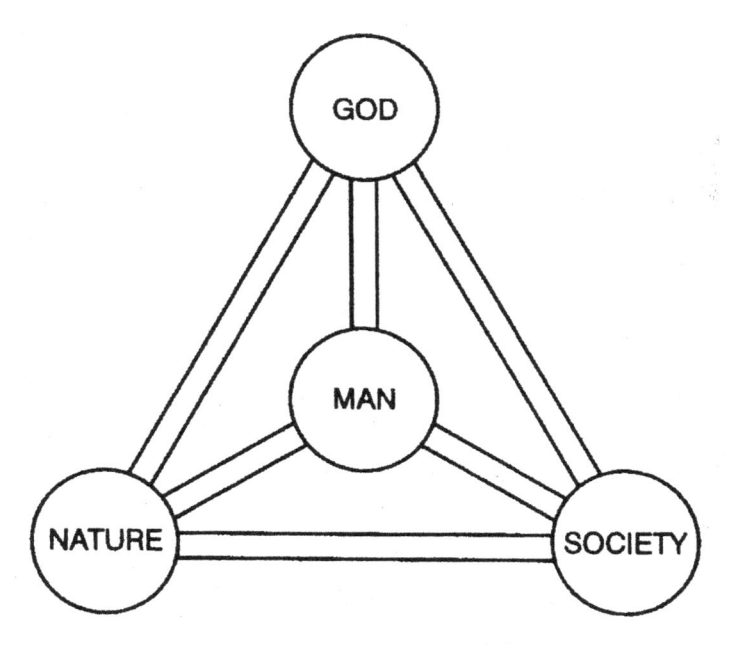

Figure 23: The Human Trinity

In this figure, there should be a harmonised two-way flow through all the channels, and ultimately all are but different expressions of the same One. Here are represented three fundamental polarities as far as individual man is concerned. They could be verbally formulated as follows.

Man in Nature is at the same time Nature in Man, since Man is Nature humanised by the course of evolution of consciousness. Thus he may appear to be a spatial object among other spatial objects to the limited Understanding that is not irradiated by Reason. However, nature is at the same time but an aspect of the total individual.

Similarly, Man in Society is at the same time Society in Man, since Man is Society individualised by the course of evolution of consciousness. Thus he may appear to be an isolated being among other isolated beings to the limited Understanding that is not irradiated by Reason. However, society is at the same time but an aspect of the total individual.

And also, Man in God is at the same time God in Man, since Man is God expressed as a unique "divine spark" revealing itself by the course of the evolution of consciousness. Thus he may appear to be an insignificant creature among other insignificant creatures to the limited Understanding that is not irradiated by Reason. However, God is at the same time but an aspect of the total individual – albeit the foundation and root of his being.

This three-fold polarity demonstrates itself in the way that, to the evolving individual consciousness, "external" reality mirrors the "internal" condition. Our environment mirrors our own face to ourselves – the problems that appear to beset us are of our own making – for there is no "inner" opposed to "outer", or "subjective" opposed to "objective", but one create reality.

For this reason Coleridge directed his readers to a study of the Bible, in that in the Old and New Testaments, the unified reality is more apparent. To the limited Understanding that is not irradiated by Reason, the events recorded are but annals of history, myth or legend to be intellectually assessed and evaluated as to their "objective" truth. Whatever residue is left after this critical process is then the substance of conventional religious or scientific belief.

However, looking at the texts with the higher Understanding irradiated by Reason, a higher truth emerges whereby the events recorded are realities and symbols mutually illuminating one another – and the act of perceiving this is an act of faith that strengthens and perpetuates itself by its own activity.

Belief is a matter of rational judgment based on evidence. Faith is an act of will; an act of fidelity to our own spiritual being.

When the lower Understanding rejects the light of Reason, it refutes the ground of its own being, and ultimately is a denial of one's own humanity. These are matters of conscience and will – not an "objective" assessment of "external" evidence of the senses.

Coleridge's conviction was, however, that if we approach the Bible in particular with our Understanding irradiated by Reason – that is, faith in it as a revelation of God to and through man – then we will apprehend its wisdom as well as its history.

He even urged his readers to "an especial study of the Old Testament as teaching the elements of political science, in the same sense as we refer to Euclid for the elements of the science of geometry."

This may sound as rather out-dated pious views of yesteryear to the modern mind; however, secular 20th century political attitudes have hardly showed themselves to be panaceas for universal happiness yet.

It is a matter that it is fruitless to argue about. As in all matters of faith, it can only be experienced, given "a willing suspension of disbelief" as Coleridge says elsewhere.

The true importance of Coleridge ultimately rests therefore, not necessarily in our struggling intellectually to comprehend his fragmented philosophical views – but in his pointing to a method whereby we ourselves can prove to ourselves, by reading in faith the annals of the "sacred book of our race", wherein the major events are seen to be also symbols, or epiphanies, or sacramental acts.

For it is this unification of the natural, the divine, and the social in our own life expression that is the goal of our own individual evolution. And by our own individual evolution we approach closer to the true expression of the will and love of God and can enter into harmonious relationships with other human beings and the whole concourse of nature.

From fall from the Garden of Eden to revelation of the New Jerusalem – with the Incarnation as the central point – the whole of life is there for whoever has "eyes to see and ears to hear."

Originally published in Quadriga 17, 18 & 20: Spring, Summer & Winter 1981

7

the impact of psychology on esoteric societies

THERE IS an ill-defined and indeed shifting boundary between the practical concerns of the occultist and the psychotherapist. This is perhaps not so surprising.

Even our awareness of the physical world through the outward senses of perception raises deep philosophical questions to which we still do not know the answers, despite our skills with neurological mechanisms. The questions (let alone the answers) are even more problematical when we try to account for "inner" experiences or motivations, of whatever kind.

Sigmund Freud anticipated some of the problems, and possibly tried to evade them, when he warned C.G.Jung about the dangers of clinical psychology sinking into the "black mud" of occultism. Psychologists of various persuasions will have their own views about all this but it may help to give a view from the swamp, so to speak, and see how things looked to the occultists, and particularly to those with a psychological bent.

Prominent among these was Dion Fortune, whose occult development more or less coincided with the rise to popular awareness of modern psychology and its analytic techniques. Born in 1890, she was a woman in her early twenties when psychoanalysis became something of a craze. This followed upon the publication of Freud's *Interpretation of Dreams* in 1900, shortly followed by *The Psychopathology of Everyday Life* and *Wit in Relation to the Unconscious*, which brought what had been a clinical subject to popular awareness.

Such an impact did these ideas make that Dion Fortune, or Miss Violet Mary Firth as she then was, could find her services very much in demand as a "lay analyst" in London, although a medically unqualified 23-year-old. She worked out of a medico-psychological clinic in Brunswick Square that appears to have been under the jurisdiction of the London (Royal Free Hospital) School of Medicine for Women, and attended relevant external courses at the University of London.

In the course of time the British Medical Association felt that things should be brought under closer control and the practice of psychoanalysis was reserved to medically qualified practitioners, which in effect put an early end to Miss Firth's promising career, although it seems likely that she would in any case have soon drifted from the paths of orthodoxy.

This was in part due to her having begun to have some odd psychological experiences that were difficult to account for in terms of accepted medical and psychological theory. These commenced at a club for students of Theosophy, which she had joined because of its convenient location to her clinic and its superior catering facilities. One day she attended one of its meditation classes in a mood that she describes as "one of mischief rather than enquiry" only to find herself experiencing thought transference, which brought her to the conclusion that if telepathy was a fact of life then it ought to have a bearing on psychotherapy; perhaps as an alternative to the lengthy, painful and cumbersome process of psychoanalysis.

At the outbreak of the war she went off to take up war work, first on the land and then in a food science research laboratory. During this time she had ample opportunity to venture inwards and the visionary experiences so induced led her towards a greater study of occult theory which in turn brought a deepening and widening of experience of apparent memories of past lives, contacts with beneficent entities, and all the worst that Freud had warned against.

In seeking to bring the two worlds together, she studied under Dr Theodore Moriarty, whom she may have originally met at the Brunswick Square clinic. Moriarty was not a doctor of medicine but he was evidently a man of some charisma as well as occult and psychological knowledge. He became in fact the model for a series of short stories that she wrote for the *Royal Magazine* that were later published in volume form as *The Secrets of Dr Taverner*. The stories purport to be written up from the casebook of a mysterious doctor who ran a private nursing home that specialised in cases beyond the reach and understanding of current medical psychology. The patients included vampires, werewolves, elemental changelings, victims of black magic and the like.

Dion Fortune claimed that she had written the stories "down" to make them acceptable to the general public, rather than hyping them up. However, this must be taken with something of a grain of salt. She was certainly capable of telling a good story by an amalgamation of some of the more odd-ball cases that she had come across at the London clinic together with occult interpretation or speculation provided by Moriarty's teaching. Moriarty never had a nursing home of the type described but he was the leader of a group of students who met together from time to time on a residential basis.

Her involvement with Moriarty did not prevent her from casting her net wide and in 1919 she also became initiated into a lodge of the Hermetic Order of the Golden Dawn, later to form her own group, which was initially intended as a kind of "outer court" to the Golden Dawn but which soon took on independent status and became a powerful fraternity in its own right. Through all of this she retained her interest in psychology and wrote some early books on the subject, either as Violet Firth or as Dion Fortune. The very titles indicate their era: *Machinery of the Mind*, *The Problem of Purity*, *The Psychology of the Servant Problem*. The last of her titles in this genre uncompromisingly incorporated her occult interests. This was *The Esoteric Philosophy of Love and Marriage* and although it is regarded with some levity in the climate of modern times it was taken very seriously in its day by her superiors in the Golden Dawn on the grounds that it betrayed "esoteric secrets".

The occultists of the later nineteenth century were obsessed with secrecy, an attitude which persisted well into the twentieth century, and it was not entirely without good reason. For instance, Dr Wynn Westcott, a London coroner, was threatened with loss of his professional post because he was a member of the Golden Dawn. A large part of this attitude was however part of the general tenor of sexual repression of the period and the realisation by those who had a practical acquaintance with magical psychodynamics that they depended upon what some psychologists call the libido, or which in oriental yoga is termed the *kundalini* or "serpent power".

In more general terms it is the life force that wells up into human creativity and that can be expressed in a variety of ways.

However, as Freud discovered in his early clinical work, there is a phenomenon known as "transference" whereby the patient may transfer sexual or other emotions upon the analyst. Insofar that some types of occult practice are broadly similar to those of psychoanalysis (free fantasy for example), it follows that "transference" can also occur in occult circles. Indeed I have heard it taken for granted by those on the wilder shores of occultism. And it has also been expressed to me by an experienced analyst that "transference" is inevitable in any analysis. This of course does not imply that occultists or psychoanalysts lead lives of sexual promiscuity.

All this was enough to cause a certain call for discretion amongst responsible occultists, although Dion Fortune tried to put a wider awareness of it to positive good use. This was a time of campaigning for sexual liberation; and freedom of information by many intellectuals, from Dr Marie Stopes on the one hand to D.H.Lawrence on the other. And when we speak of these matters we have to try to imagine ourselves back to rigid and inhibited attitudes and assumptions that would be quite unthinkable nowadays. Whether the lower classes should be instructed in the existence, let alone the methods of contraception. Or whether residential domestic servant girls should be allowed to have "followers" or boyfriends on their few hours off – part of the much discussed "servant problem" to which Dion Fortune had devoted an early book.

Dion Fortune later strove to open up the subject in the guise of fiction, and so the writings of her mature years can be divided into two complementary sectors. On the one hand non-fiction works explaining the general philosophy and theory of occultism (e.g. *The Esoteric Orders and their Work*, *The Training and Work of an Initiate*, *The Mystical Qabalah*, etc.); and on the other hand the novels, which have a story line elucidating principles of psychic polarity between hero and heroine (e.g. *The Winged Bull*, *The Goat-foot God*, *The Sea Priestess*, *Moon Magic*.)

The heroes of her books therefore tend to be somewhat repressed men, ill used by society, whose creativity is released with the help of a woman. This is achieved by directing their mutual desires through a subtlety of psychic interplay to open up inner depths that bring a fulfilment that may or may not then be expressed physically by the act of love. There is something of the popular romantic novel in all of this, although her works would certainly never have been quite suitable for the publishing list of Mills and Boon. Her intentions were also to reawaken the knowledge and technique of the ancient mystery religions as a method of individual and social healing in modern times.

In an article in her society's magazine she wrote, "My novels have a purpose, which is the purpose of initiation ... they are closely akin to the initiation dramas of the ancient Mysteries, in that they take the reader by way of dramatic representations to a realisation of the nature of the soul."

It was her original intention to write a whole series of such novels, possibly ten in number, corresponding to the ten spheres of the Tree of Life of the Qabalah. As she said, "*The Mystical Qabalah* gives the theory but the novels give the practice." Furthermore, "Point by point I am taking the great problems of human life, analysing them in characters' experiences, and finding the ultimate happy ending in a definite practical psycho-magical solution – showing exactly how it was done so that anybody with a similar problem can go and do likewise."

It was perhaps, in practice, not quite so simple as that, but in the general run of her intentions we seem to be coming close to elements of C.G.Jung's analytical psychology. His favoured sources were to be found in mythology, legend and ancient mystery traditions, including even alchemy, which were also the pabulum for Dion Fortune's aims.

C.G.Jung's works, when they became available in English, certainly had a considerable impact upon her. Jungian psychology seemed an excellent way of "explaining" occultism to the outside world. And it was certainly something of a fillip to respectability to have an eminent psychologist talking in similar terms to the occultists.

Bernard Bromage, an occult commentator of respected integrity, interviewed Dion Fortune at about this time and found her full of psychological terminology. This led him to write that she "had attained the greater part of her knowledge of magical techniques solely by study of psychological principles ... She had attended many courses at ... the University of London, in such related subjects as psychology, psychoanalysis, mental therapy and the like, and she tended to use the terminology employed in these circles in what seemed to me a rather over-facile and slightly too credulous manner. She was full of 'ab-reactions', 'compulsive neuroses', 'psychosomatic conditions' and the like."

Part of this emphasis may have been put on for Bromage's benefit, and when the article was published, many years later, in *Light* magazine in 1960, some of those who had known Dion Fortune intimately found his pen portrait unreal to the point of hilarity. The point being that psychological terms can play a useful part in presenting some of the dynamics of the magical philosophy in a way that is likely to be more readily understood, and Dion Fortune no doubt made the most of this, as I and no doubt many others have done when faced with media interviewers.

Convenient though it may be as a type of shorthand, it is nonetheless misleading, although perhaps just how misleading is perhaps not readily apparent. William G. Gray performed an important service when in his occult books, from *Magical Ritual Methods* onwards, he drew attention to the fourfold structure of practical occult symbolism in its own right, without recourse to Jungian psychological interpretations. The fourfold system had been there for all to see of course, from time immemorial, in Celtic legend, the Tarot, the Amerindian medicine wheel, the Tibetan Book of the Dead and so on. Indeed there is a certain circularity in the process in that the term "mandala" coined by Jung for a symbol of psychological integration, means in fact "magic circle". However, whether Jung means quite the same thing by the term as the occultists is somewhat open to question.

At root the occult and the psychological premises differ very considerably, and we have to ask ourselves very carefully how far the "collective unconscious" equates with the "astral plane" and whether the "Self" is the same as the "Divine Spark", or how far the "Anima" resembles the "Holy Guardian Angel", and whether the "Masters of the Wisdom" are manifestations of the "Animus" in the female medium.

However, there was sufficient evident similarity for Dion Fortune to encourage the members of her society in the study of Jungian psychology, and until at least the late 1950s a book on the subject, by Jacobi, was part of the curriculum for all intending members. It was indeed the aim for some time to try to have at least one member trained in Jungian analysis in order to provide a service for members in the resolution of any psychological problems, which can become acute in the forcing house of a working occult group. However, there was a tendency for those who took up such training to leave the ranks and not return. There was clearly some kind of undefined chasm, between allegiance to Jungian psychology and allegiance to the occult society, that was not easily bridged. In later years, the reverse was known to happen, of at least one Jungian psychologist coming to the occult fold, and then ceasing to practise. In the end the society turned to other forms of therapy for the benefit of its members.

Israel Regardie, a contemporary of Dion Fortune, whose occult writings gained a wide following, was also much influenced by the Jungian psychology, and his early books lean heavily on psychological interpretations of magical dynamics. He had something of an irascible streak and was roundly contemptuous of the tradition of contact with superior spiritual intelligences. He castigated all who sought "that commonly found fantasy ... of being in touch with Masters", which, he averred, "is so evidently neurotic, or even blatantly delusional, that most of those claiming it would have done better to have included some kind of psychotherapy in their magical training."

Dion Fortune, who certainly did believe in that "commonly found fantasy", and practised it, nonetheless also felt that "some kind of psychotherapy would be an advantage in magical training" and went some way towards trying to implement it, as we have described. Regardie did modify his views somewhat in later years, although of course much of the alleged communications put about by various "channels" merits the full force of his polemic. What he called the "inepti" outnumber the "adepti" very considerably.

Regardie himself went on to other forms of psychology and became a practitioner of the techniques of Wilhelm Reich. Dion Fortune's society also switched away from an emphasis on the Jungian psychology to look at alternative forms of psychotherapeutics. There was considerable interest in L. Ron Hubbard's "dianetics" when it first came out, in the 1950s, later to develop into "scientology". This movement has had something of a bad press in one way and another but in its early days senior members of the Society of the Inner Light took a lot of trouble to study it. Once again, as with the Jungian interface, some did not return. However, for some time elementary psychotherapeutic techniques from this system were provided for members, either in group sessions or for individuals. I experienced some of this myself and have to say I found it nothing but beneficial.

However, it was a phase that passed and the society developed a less psychological and more mystical orientation, while at the same time producing some perceptive instruction on "spiritual pathologies" in which psychological insights were intimately bound up with occult and mystical dynamics.

As an example of this new approach, greater emphasis was placed upon the ability and indeed the will of the spirit to express itself efficiently and intelligently in the world. It was recognised that many seekers after the higher wisdom do so partly on false pretences, not as elevated souls seeking to give selfless service to humanity, but as reluctant and inadequate citizens of the cosmos in full retreat from the problems and responsibilities of material expression.

Typical symptoms of such a spiritual pathology would include:

1: difficulty in finishing a job or a cycle of activity completely; giving an impression of other-worldliness or spiritual "top heaviness";
2: a reincarnationary record demonstrating sequences of lives spent withdrawn in religious or occult orders, occasionally interspersed with a life of extreme violence – in short, lack of balance in life expression;
3: a mind dominating the feelings, thus having no real warmth of "heart", even when outwardly apparently kind and considerate;
4: difficulties in relating to the opposite sex because of a compulsion to be independent, aloof, self-sufficient;
5: a tendency to be unmarried, or else married to a similar type, with little interest in children or domestic or family life;
6: very often in the right, but intolerant of imperfections in others or themselves;
7: at heart lonely and unfulfilled, seeking "higher" consciousness to compensate for the hollowness of expression and experience at the lower levels.

In such an approach as this, the Society of the Inner Light would appear to have developed a mode of psychological analysis particularly related to their own field of endeavour, and also incorporating their own assumptions as to the importance of the spiritual element in human psychology, and to the phenomenon of reincarnation. And when we come to look at the esoteric field generally, there has been a tendency to pursue lines of psychological analysis in similar fashion. Thus it would seem that, for the committed and experienced occultist, the Jungian and Freudian orthodoxies leave something to be desired. This is most readily apparent in the question of "Masters" on the one hand, and reincarnation theory on the other.

There remains however a considerable margin of overlap, both in theory and practice, and even in intention in that much "New Age" interest in occult dynamics is geared to psychotherapeutic aims; that is, to the resolution of personal problems and the integration of the personality as ends in themselves. We may even see psychologists using esoteric techniques and "maps of the soul" as a means of therapy. For instance, the "psychosynthesis" of Dr Roberto Assagioli bears much similarity to the esoteric psychology and cosmic groundplan of Alice A. Bailey, who in turn derives her inspiration from H.P.Blavatsky, the founding Theosophist. Indeed, it is a moot point as to who used "free association" or "free fantasy" first, the psychologists or the occultists. The latter tend to call it "path working" or "scrying in the spirit vision", although there is a latter day halfway house in the term "initiated symbol projection".

Various other esoteric themes have permeated the psychotherapeutic sphere. There is, for instance, the Enneagram, favoured by Gurdjieff and Ouspensky and their followers. This is a device like a nine-pointed star that serves as the ground plan for an esoteric cosmology and general yardstick of inner and outer experience, in much the same way that the Qabalistic Tree of Life or the Twelvefold Circle of the Zodiac is utilised by other occultists. One may nowadays find Roman Catholic pastors using it as the basis for psychotherapeutic workshops and also linking it to more objective mystical and religious principles such as the personality of Jesus Christ or to the personal prayer life. Of course the enneagram does have an esoteric and religious origin in that it comes down to us from or through the medieval Sufis, and possibly from Pythagorean number mysticism before that.

We therefore find that as well as there being several schools of clinical psychology there are also various schools of esoteric psychology. And when we come to practical experience we find that the theoretical assumptions of the practitioners seem to influence the results and to dominate their interpretation. It has been observed before that the different schools of psychology seem to develop self-validating experience. Freudian patients come up with Freudian symbolism, Jungian patients oblige with Jungian, and so on. The same might be said about the various schools of occultism.

This does not necessarily mean that all involved, on either side, are dishonest or deluded. Materialist critics with their own reductionist preconceptions also affect, or inhibit, the results they try to observe, even if they like to think that they are the only ones who are "truly objective". (In fact, in this field, it is probable that this question-begging term is quite meaningless.) There is nothing quite so pathetic as the sight of an anthropologist, for example, fluttering like a moth against a lighted window, struggling to get in to the lighted world of spiritual experience, the restraining glass being their own academic assumptions. Jungian psychologists, to the occultist, seem to occupy an intermediate position; the window is open, but they will not come all the way in!

A lot of the problem of intercommunication stems from a lack of well defined terms and also from the related problem of an unsound philosophical basis upon which to measure the subjective and the objective and their inter-relationship. It is possible that the greatest contribution to solving these problems has been with us for more than 150 years but has not been recognised yet. This is the epistemological ontology of Samuel Taylor Coleridge.

Unfortunately he never quite got round to expounding this concisely and systematically, but it has been reconstituted to some degree by Owen Barfield, in his monumental work, *What Coleridge Thought*. Barfield was a close lifelong friend of C.S.Lewis and J.R.R.Tolkien, and one of that famous discussion group "the Inklings". As a proselyte of the thought of Rudolf Steiner, he was for long highly regarded in anthroposophical circles,and latterly increasingly encouraged and respected in American academe.

I have endeavoured to show something of the modern relevance of Coleridge's thought and its subtle and far-reaching ramifications in *Magic and the Western Mind* (now republished under its original title, *A History of White Magic*), and in more detail in *The Magical World of the Inklings*, although Owen Barfield's work, whilst not perhaps being too easy to read, is certainly more profound. Ultimately, of course, one has to go to Coleridge himself, a prodigy whose youthful reading included Plato, Plotinus, Giordano Bruno and Marsilio Ficino, for the most part in the original, and who later travelled in Germany and learnt the language to study the roots of the romantic tradition, which includes the contributions of the Rosicrucian based mystic Jacob Boehme on the one hand and the poet, philosopher and scientist Johann Wolfgang von Goethe on the other.

Most of these trends point to the fact that, in the last analysis, human psychology cannot be understood without recourse to the spark of divinity in man. And if, in our modern prejudice, we prefer to leave out the personal term "God", then we may, for want of something better, perhaps utilise the concept of Pure Reason that served Plotinus. This is the "lux interna" that infuses the imagination with inspiration, and the concrete understanding with intuitive insights. In Coleridge's imagery it is the Promethean fire that was stolen from heaven and which we have not yet learnt how to handle — what Existentialists have called the challenge to accept our freedom. This also implies a dreadful responsibility, but one which we may, like cosmic adolescents, learn how to grow into without too much hooliganism.

It is this concept of the evolution of consciousness that Barfield illustrates in the light of Coleridge's thought. We have a parallel from the psychological side represented in such works as Erich Neumann's *History and Origins of Consciousness* and *The Great Mother*. Here we have the lineaments of the growth of human spiritual awareness and responsibility from the group consciousness and "participation mystique" of animal man, through the individual ego development represented by the myths and legends of the hero, to our present dilemma of what to do with our quasi-divine powers in the fields of ecology, genetics, nuclear power, and so on.

Psychology has done much in this respect to point the way, but still has a tendency to confine the extent of the cosmos to the contents of the human skull. If we need the help of spirits from the vasty deep, they may well speak to us through our intuitive and imaginative antennae, but they are likely to be rather more than archetypes of the unconscious. This is a thought that is so profound in its implications that we might well feel a great deal safer within a psychological subjective bunker should such spirits turn out to be not "goodies" but "baddies". And indeed, demonology and the constitution of the angelic hierarchies have somewhat fallen out of fashion during the current epoch. This does not necessarily imply that they, any more than God, have been annihilated by our ostrich-like posture.

As a balanced way of coming to terms with the problems involved, perhaps a synthesis between the occult and psychological positions might be found, whether or not it is good practice to build permanent houses upon bridges. One example of such an approach may be found in *The Inner Guide Meditation* of Edwin Steinbrecher. This is a system that combines psychological dynamics with the astrological birth chart, the meditational consequences of which are conversations with helpful beings as represented by standardised Tarot images.

The symbolic mechanism is based upon the Golden Dawn system of attributions between astrological planet, constellation or element on the one hand, and Tarot Trump image on the other. There are arguments that this system is largely arbitrary but in the light of experience this is no great objection to virtually any system of occult symbolism. If correspondences are believed in, and worked out in a reasonably balanced and consistent way, then the chances are that they will work. William Blake provides an example of this, with his endless identification of Biblical locations with parts of London or "Albion" in general, along with tribes and patriarchs of the ancient Hebrews and representative figures within his own personal life (such as the soldier who accused him of treason). They may be arbitrary but they are not inconsequential. Whoever is prepared to work with them sympathetically will find that they work. And it follows that if one prefers to modify them, or to substitute one's own system entirely, then that too is likely to work.

For Steinbrecher's students, starting off in visualisation of Plato's cave, and being guided by an animal (a personal totem), one may be led to a communion with the representation of the Sun in glory of the Tarot Trumps. From this healing and integrating contact one may be passed on to others, and the whole thing may eventually be worked out in terms of the configuration of the astrological birth chart, with relevance to personal life history and relationships. This, it may be judged, is both psychology and occultism.

We have noted that a fundamental divide between the occult and the psychological approaches is two-fold:

i) an objective recognition of superior spiritual beings, and
ii) process of reincarnation of the soul.

As an illustration of the type of psychology into which these occult assumptions may lead us, we can examine "an anatomy of the subtle bodies" promulgated by Dion Fortune in 1940, well after she had become familiar with Jungian interpretations. These ideas were published in her society's magazine as part of a series entitled Words of the Masters, indicating that they are attributed to a higher external source than the personal theories of the writer. Here Figure 24 may prove helpful to clarify the essential concept from the detail.

We have a threefold spiritual entity, commonly called the Higher Self, or Individuality, that is cosmically self determined, and so fundamentally harmonious, and which expresses a particular spiritual "Ray", "harmonic" or "archetype." This unit is responsible for building a series of incarnations within the lower worlds of ideas, feelings, sensations. In this sense it has a sort of architectural role in relation to the lower bodies, which ideally are the temple of the spirit. These lower bodies are represented by the projected Personality or Lower Self, which is shown in anthropological shape in the diagram, as opposed to the star-like configuration of the Individuality or Higher Self.

The problem now lies in the means of communication between these two expressions of a single human being: the Higher with its background of harmonious cosmic eternity; and the Lower, developed in the familiar way within the world, subject to heredity, genetics and environmental conditioning. In this 1940 teaching, there is put forward an additional two-fold connection, one called the Fate and the other the Ghost.

The Fate is described as the abstract essence of the past, acting as a causative agent upon the current Personality. It is therefore experienced as a "force of destiny" or our own especial mode of expression which leads us to inner fulfilment and outward expression of our own unique potentiality, which will be an amalgam of basic spiritual type together with the abstracted experience of previous lives on earth or of more direct cosmic experience in the higher worlds.

The Ghost, on the other hand, is an image of the ego of the last incarnation, and it contains within it, rather like a nest of Chinese boxes, or a succession of mirror reflections, previous ego images. Its attributes, then, are to provide a composite picture of memories of previous form experience. Although itself never more than one incarnation old, it contains memory images of the previous ghost and so on down the time track. But whereas the Higher Self contains the integrated and harmonised realisations of past form experience, the Ghost is a repository of unassimilated experience, and is thus similar in nature to the subconscious of the current Personality, and in its remoter memory images to the Jungian collective unconscious.

It will be seen from the diagram that both Fate and Ghost have different relationships with Individuality and Personality. The Fate is, in a sense, a channel itself, between the two sets of vehicles. The Ghost, on the other hand, is more of an extraneous appendage. It can have a determining influence upon the Personality, perhaps over-riding that of the Fate, whilst it also has a tenuous link with the Individuality, without which it would become a completely dissociated shell. It is by no means an evil entity when in touch with the spiritual life of the Individuality (which is in a sense ultimately responsible for it), but it tends towards the past, and to unresolved problems of the past, as opposed to the Fate, which looks toward fruitful growth, new experience, and to the future.

This has an important bearing upon occult techniques and training methods, the aim of which should be to open up Personality consciousness to the Individuality, via the Fate, rather than to the drag from the past represented by the Ghost. One may see herein the reason why mainstream esoteric teaching from the responsible schools heads students away from undue interest in past incarnations. Wherever such is not delusory speculation, or pandering to a hypnotist's will, it is liable only to set up a drag from unresolved problems of the past, particularly if the "memories" are

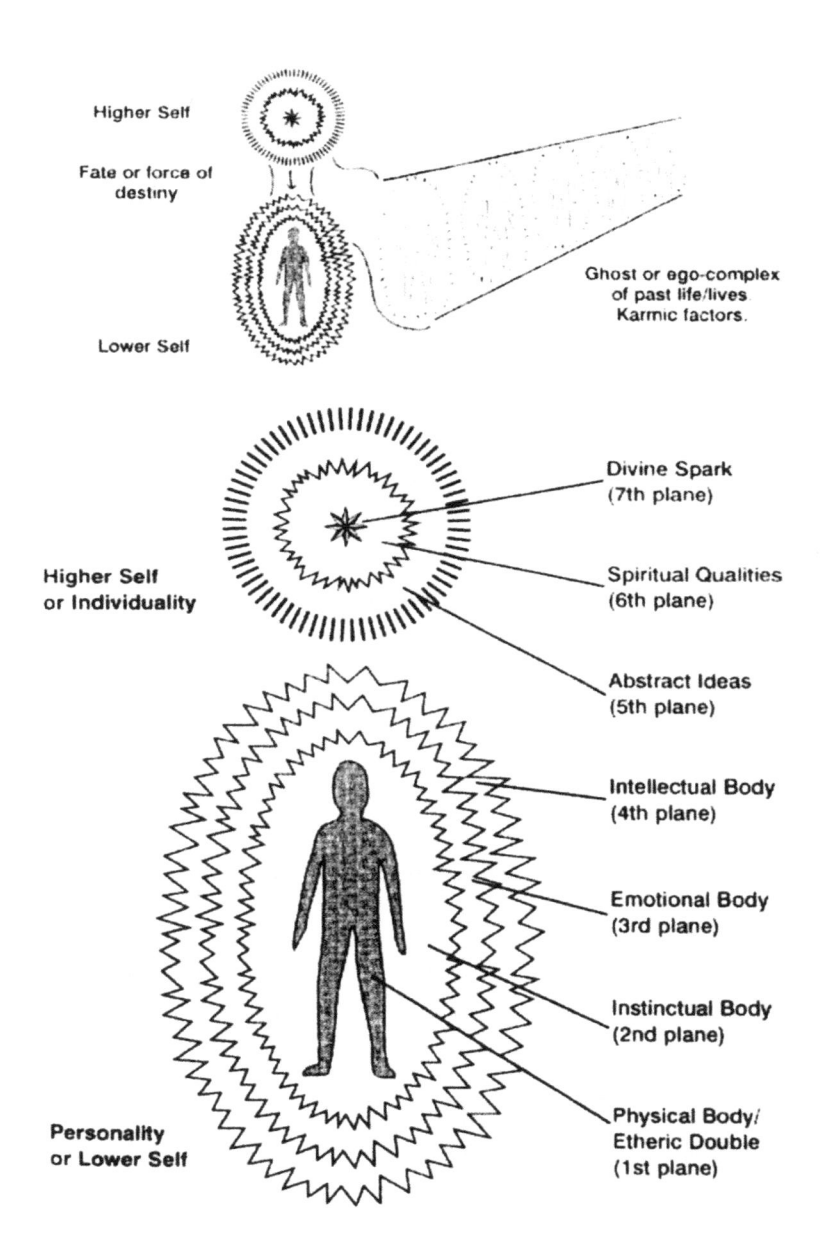

Figure 24: The Fate and the Ghost

cloaked in glamour and self admiration. This is in fact but another form of spiritual pathology.

It might be thought that stirring about in the past in this way was a means of relieving or releasing or abreacting past repressions. This is a point of view, and in line with Freudian aims and techniques. The more positive pursuit of the strengthening of the influence of the Fate is however an integrative approach that in the psychological field characterises the approach of Jung.

Enhanced contact with the Individuality ought to be an act of positive achievement and healing, and this is borne out in other schools of esoteric thought. We have been looking at the human psyche in spiritual extension in terms of Dion Fortune's teaching. Much the same pattern may be found in the esoteric psychology of Alice A. Bailey, which in turn derives from H.P.Blavatsky and traditional oriental sources. For instance, Dion Fortune's concepts of the Individuality or Higher Self, in Alice Bailey's works are called the Soul. And Dion Fortune's identification of the Fate as a channel between Higher and Lower Selves has close correspondence with Alice Bailey's *antahkarana* or "rainbow bridge". Furthermore, the memory images of the Ghost are another way of looking at the Theosophical conception of Seed Atoms. It will be gathered that esoteric psychology is no simplistic panacea, but rather adds dimensions onto the more rudimentary conceptions of conventional psychology.

It may therefore be of interest if we take an actual case history, and we have one more or less in the public domain, in the life and work of Dion Fortune herself. We may find, for example, some exemplifications of the Ghost in the comments she made on her later novels, *The Sea Priestess* and *Moon Magic*, for the protagonist of these two novels has many attributes that suggest she might well be a manifestation of Dion Fortune's own Ghost. In her preface to *Moon Magic* for instance, she writes, "when I imagined the character of Vivien Le Fay Morgan, or Lilith Le Fay, as she variously called herself, I brought into being a personality ... she is very far from being a puppet in my hands, but takes charge of the situation." And "After the conclusion of *The Sea Priestess* she would not lie quiet in her grave, but her ghost persisted in walking. It walked to such good purpose that it forced upon me the writing of this book."

After several abortive attempts at writing a sequel to the first novel, she finally set the narrative in the first person, allowing the heroine to, so to speak, write it herself, whereupon, she reports, the book more or less wrote itself. As to the final result, she records "I have not a very high opinion of it as literature but it is certainly a psychological curio. It contains, moreover, an amount of very odd lore, much of which I did not know anything about until I read it in these pages."

"What have I created in Lilith Le Fay?" she asks, "Who and what is Lilith, and why did she live on after the book about her was finished (i.e. *The Sea Priestess*), and insist on appearing again? (i.e. in *Moon Magic*). Have I furnished myself with a dark familiar?"

It is of course not uncommon for authors to find characters taking on life of their own in any story, and a similar phenomenon can happen to actors. In many cases it is felt that this gives a sense of vitality to their work. It is, of course, in either case, an example of the "magical" use of the imagination, or in popular psychological parlance, "working off the subconscious."

However, we enter a further dimension when such characters become compulsive or obsessive in their effect, or take on a more objective reality. And in the case of Dion Fortune and her fictional heroine it seems that we are moving into this area when she writes, "Lilith lives after a curious manner of her own; she lives for others as well as for me; and it may well be that to some of those who read these pages she will come as a shadowy figure half-seen in the twilight of the mind."

It should be said that such a visitation is not likely to be tremendously helpful, as an examination of the character of this figure may show. We could, for example, take our previous checklist of symptoms of spiritual pathology and see what evidence there is for "otherworldliness," "spiritual top-heaviness," "lack of warmth," "mind-dominated feelings," "aloofness and self sufficiency, particularly in relation to the opposite sex," "lack of interest in children or domestic ties," "intolerance of imperfection," and an "inner hollowness." It should be clear, that on the evidence of the novels, Miss Lilith Le Fay does not score very well as a rounded human being.

She undoubtedly is a lady of some charisma and power, and she is certainly well intentioned, but nonetheless all her relations with the men she selects are power seeking and manipulative. She is therefore not an evil person but a profoundly out-dated one, and her vitality stems not from what she is but from what she knows. Her own justification for her actions would be that the current age is in need of some of the ancient wisdom which she has to teach, but it is arguable that she also could have benefited if she had lived a more complete and whole life in the world as she found it.

Conventional psychologists might interpret the action of *Moon Magic* in terms of Dion Fortune's unsuccessful marriage. In 1927 she married Dr Thomas Penry Evans, whom some consider to be, in character, somewhat similar to the Dr Rupert Malcolm of the novel, but the relationship had foundered by 1939. Alan Richardson, in his biography of Dion Fortune, *Priestess*, deals with the situation from this point of view in some detail, but with the proviso that "we should beware of dismissing her ideas on sexuality as 'nothing more than' a matter of compensation. She had these ideas all her lives."

Mr Richardson's use of the plural is significant to our thesis, in that the heroine of *Moon Magic* is at least in part an expression of Dion Fortune's Ghost, with its reflected memories of past incarnations. However, rather than dwell upon this manifestation of unequilibrated experience from the past, let us look to the other side of the coin and try to discern the influence of Dion Fortune's Fate. This will give evidence of itself as all the good things that were achieved by Dion Fortune in her life and which have lived after her, and to this end we have an impressive catalogue.

In general terms it may be summed up by the early expressed intention to try to revivify the powers of the ancient mystery religions in the modern age, and in this she to a large part succeeded, not only in the contribution to the general consciousness of her Society of the Inner Light as an organisation in its own right, but in the influence it has spread and work that has been done by various individuals who have been trained in its methods and who have then gone on to set up their own centres of teaching and spiritual activity. This is a natural type of seeding in work of this nature, where individuals are encouraged to discern and to carve out their own pattern of destiny within the world. Thus much that can be traced back to the influence of Dion Fortune points to her own Higher Self and to her own Fate. Much of this comes through in the early textbooks and essays, with their consummate commonsense and dedicated good faith, and also again in some of the Weekly War Letters, where her courage and good humour in the light of considerable adversity and indeed physical danger reflect a Personality well expressing the Fate and the Individuality.

She was at something of a disadvantage in being lumbered with assumptions about being the withdrawn head of an enclosed order, and in this she was as much a victim of the expectations of her disciples as of her own predilections. It is her husband, Dr Penry Evans, who perhaps finds his way as an initiate in the world with rather more success. As Alan Richardson says, "Merl had several masks: he was the Sun Priest, he was a physician; he lived his life through many outlets, none of them really overlapping." He had been one of the first to volunteer at the outbreak of war in 1914, and after active service in the Artists Rifles and the Machine Gun Corps, left with the rank of 2nd Lieutenant. He studied medicine and qualified as a doctor in 1924, when he took on a "house job" at Charing Cross Hospital, followed by positions in public health in East Ham. He met and married Dion Fortune with whom he developed his esoteric side, but rather than become an enclosed adept he went on to run his own factory engaged in research into health foods based on soya bean products. When civil war broke out in Spain he worked on the republican side to try to alleviate problems of malnutrition in children. After having to fly for his life from General Franco, abandoning all his medical equipment in Barcelona, he became Assistant Tuberculosis Officer for Southwark before eventually becoming Medical Officer for Health for Beaconsfield, where he designed his own house (called Pan) and settled down with the second Mrs Penry Evans. In his latter years he was described as "a man that was happy with life, very droll and kind, quite passionate about music and possessed of a very definite charisma – a kind and kingly presence."

So we find in Dr Penry Evans an example of an esoterically minded idealist who was at the same time able to a large degree to express his ideals in the world. And as we have mentioned above, there was in the War Letters of Dion Fortune (which have been published, in part, as *The Magical Battle of Britain*) particular evidence of a commonsensical, humorous and compassionate woman of the world, concerned with political and social issues, and by no means the encloistered femme fatale of the image of the novels.

As she writes elsewhere, the Higher Self may tend to come through to greater contact in times of physical danger, and in this respect the letters to her students, during the dark days of 1940 during the London blitz, may give a closer idea of the Individuality of Dion Fortune as expressed through a dedicated Personality.

For instance, after being bombed out of her headquarters in October 1940 she can write:

> "In our last letter we asked our members and friends to invoke for protection of 3 Queensborough Terrace and in this letter we have the ironical task of informing them that we have been bombed out of it, though without casualties; so it may be maintained that the invocation was at least a partial success, though your Leader and her Librarian look like a couple of sweeps owing to a difference of opinion with the roof, which fell in on them, but tactfully refrained from hitting them.
>
> "It has often been alleged that Dion Fortune is a Black Occultist, and we regretfully admit that the allegation can no longer be denied; however it is hoped that soap and water will restore her to the Right Hand Path and her students will once more be able to hold up their heads before a world always too ready to think the worst."

Thus we trust that we have made a sufficiently clear demonstration of the two concepts of the Fate and the Ghost, at any rate as they impinge upon and influence the expression of the Personality within the world. The more valuable exercise of course, will be for each one of us to attempt to make the distinction within our own lives.

There is, however, a further element from which we should not shrink in any discussion of the difference between the occult and the psychological points of view. This is the degree of objectivity of thought-forms.

As Dion Fortune remarked in her preface to *Moon Magic*, others besides herself had become conscious of the figure of Lilith Le Fay. She also says, in her article on the subject, that "the Ghost is not a living entity but a thought-form, and the methods of dispelling thought-forms are applicable to it." A problem may be that many occult aspirants who do not know any better might well go out of their way to invoke the thought-form, assuming it to be a power or knowledge bestowing experience. So it might be for those who have the ability to handle it but one cannot universally recommend the practice of trying to catch a tiger by the tail, or perhaps not a tiger but something more like the crowned serpent in Charles Williams' novel, *The Place of the Lion*, that dominated poor Dora Wilmot, and induced this weak and hitherto ineffectual woman to write a number of malevolent anonymous letters and then to try to coil sinuously round the gentleman who caught her at it.

A problem is that a thought form such as that of the heroine of *The Sea Priestess* and *Moon Magic*, having been built up by a powerful imaginative consciousness such as Dion Fortune undoubtedly had, will tend to be very powerful and persistent. And coming out of her own bank of "Ghost" memories it will have the validity of being based upon ancient realities, and will tend to appeal to others who have a similar bank of memories. In other words it will stimulate and reinforce their own Ghost.

This is unlikely to do them very much good. Not only does it deflect attention away from the healthy influence of the Fate, it brings yet more unbalance to bear upon the unbalance that made the thought-form seem attractive in the first place. Thus do we get a certain class of houri on the occult fringe obsessed with fantasies of "polarity" and yet never really making a start in the real business of human and social relationships. Such are also unlikely to want to accept the boring prospect of sustained training in meditation and contemplation aimed at the true contact with the spiritual dynamics of the Fate and the Higher Self. The more highly coloured exercises of the active imagination will have much more appeal, particularly if they feed the deviation.

The acid test as to whether all is well or not will be found in the circumstances of daily life – are they balanced or chaotic, are relationships sustained or promiscuous, is mental confusion evident through failure to be punctual, or emotional confusion evident through inability to be tidy? In Qabalistic terms, the ethic of Malkuth, of daily outer life, is Order, and a persistent failure in this indicates that all is not well on the higher levels, no matter what the pretensions may be.

Also, the more the thought-form is brooded upon, the more powerful does it become, which is a point of general public hygiene upon the astral plane, not just a personal psychological problem. This is an area that psychology seems unwilling to address, at least in these terms, although it may well be covered in terms of group psychology and analysis and manipulation of the public psyche through the mass media, be it in terms of advertising, or political propaganda, or more subtle ways of manipulating the "spirit of the times".

Indeed it might well be asked how far the "image making" of modern times is not a magical operation in the pure sense, of manipulating the consciousness of others through symbols and sonics. Dr Goebbels was the first modern exponent of it on a massive scale but nowadays "image making" and "spin doctoring" is almost a commonplace. Indeed we might further ask ourselves, in the way that we use the media of mass communication, how far it is possible to invoke a national Fate or Ghost.

In terms of Britain, the Fate, as channel of the Higher Self, or Folk Angel, might be regarded as Logres, the realm of King Arthur and his Round Table Knights, as C.S.Lewis has suggested. Whilst the Ghost might be found expressed in the football hooligans who invade the continent of Europe chanting xenophobic slogans. It would be an interesting point of debate to determine into which category the fighting of the Falklands war would fall.

Needless to say, every country has its own Fate or Destiny to fulfil, and its Ghost to lay. And ultimately we have to think in terms of the human race as a whole. A problem at the same time occult and psychological.

First published as "The Impact of Psychology upon Esoteric Societies" in *Psychology and the Spiritual Traditions* edited R.J.Stewart, Element Books, 1990. Slightly corrected in the light of new research in the preparation of *Dion Fortune and the Inner Light* (Thoth Publications, 2000).

index

adepthood 5, 97, 109
Adonai 31, 38
Agrippa, Cornelius 43
Albertus Magnus 35
angels 31, 36, 37, 38, 40, 41, 42, 43, 45, 46, 48, 74
Aquarian age 53
Aristotle 35, 66
Arthurian legends 55, 112
Aslan 57
Assagioli, Dr Roberto 99
astral imagination 11
astral plane 10, 96, 112
astrology 36, 83, 103
Avalon 55, 56, 57

Bacon, Francis 78, 79, 85
Bailey, Alice A. 99, 106
Barfield, Owen 70, 77, 100, 101
Bedivere 55, 56
black magic 7, 93
Blake, William 17, 76, 102
Blavatsky, H.P. 53, 99, 106
Boehme, Jacob 57, 69, 101
Book of Formation 25
Book of Splendour 27
Botticelli 43
Bromage, Bernard 95, 96
Bruno, Giordano 79, 101

Capra, Fritjof 86
Celestial Hierarchies, The 38
chakras 53
Chardin, Teilhard de 17
chariot mysticism 24-25
Christian religious experience 13
Cloud of Unknowing, The 14
Coleridge, Samuel Taylor 10, 69-89, 100, 101

Cosmic Doctrine, The 7, 12
crystalline spheres 46, 47, 48
Cube of Space 25-27

Dante 14
death 61, 62, 63
De Occulta Philosophia 43
Descartes 76, 86, 87
Descent into Hell 58
dianetics 97
Dionysius 38, 40
Divine Spark 7, 96
Doctrine of Substituted Love 58

Elijah 25
enneagram 99
Essenes and the Qabalah, The 34
evolution 5, 6, 7, 11, 17, 74
Excalibur 55, 56

Faerie Queen, The 66
Fate and Ghost 103-106, 108-112
Fellowship of the Round Table 56
Ficino, Marsilio 34-37, 43, 45, 101
Fludd, Robert 19, 28, 29, 31, 45, 46, 47, 48, 49, 50
Folk Angel 112
Fortune, Dion 6, 10, 12, 91, 92, 93, 94, 95, 96, 97, 103, 106-110
Four Elements 46, 47, 77
Four Worlds 38-45
Freud, Sigmund 91, 92, 94, 100, 106

Genesis 27
Goat-foot God, The 94
goddess 48
Golden Dawn 93, 102
Gray, William G. 96

Hermetic scripts 35
Higher Self 16, 74, 77, 103, 106, 108, 110-112
Holy Grail 18, 54
Holy Names of God 27, 29, 31, 32, 37, 46
Holy Trinity 87
Human Trinity 87

Ignatius of Loyola 13
imagination 11, 17, 62, 71, 76, 78, 81, 83, 111
initiation 6, 7, 8, 95
Initiation of the Nadir 7, 12
Inner Guide Meditation, The 102
inner plane orders 9, 10
inner science 45, 49
involution 5, 7, 10, 12
Isis of Nature 48, 49

Jehovah 29, 31, 46
Jewish mysticism 19, 21, 23, 25, 27, 28, 34, 45
Jove 82
Julian of Norwich 58
Jung, C.G. 91, 95, 96, 97, 98, 100, 103, 104, 106

Kabbalah Unveiled, The 38
King Arthur, King of Kings 55

Lamb, Charles 69
Le Fay, Lilith (Vivien Le Fay Morgan) 106, 107, 110
Lewis, C.S. 56, 57, 100, 112
Lodge, Sir Oliver 67
Logres 112
Lower Self 16, 74, 77, 103, 106
Lyrical Ballads 69

Magical Battle of Britain, The 109
Magical Ritual Methods 96
Markale, Jean 55
Masters 8, 10, 11, 96, 99, 103

Mathers, S.L. MacGregor 38
meditation 7, 13, 14, 15, 17, 18, 111
meditation of perception 14, 17
mediumship 10
Merlin 56
Mirandola, Pico della 37, 38, 45, 69
Moon Magic 94, 106, 107, 108, 110, 111
Moriarty, Dr Theodore 92, 93
Morte d'Arthur 55
Moses 23, 24, 35, 63
Moses de León 27
mystical meditation 13, 15, 16
Mystical Qabalah, The 94, 95

natural magic 36-37
Neumann, Erich 101
Newton, Sir Isaac 66, 79, 84
Noyes, Alfred 64-67

occult meditation 13, 15, 16, 17
occult secrecy 76, 93
Old Testament 23, 25, 37, 88, 89
Orphic Hymns 36

Penry Evans, Dr Thomas 108-109
Perkins, Professor David 65
Place of the Lion, The 111
Plato 35, 69, 78, 79, 85, 101, 102
Plotinus 16, 69, 101
prayer 7, 14, 99
Priestess 108
Prometheus 82, 87, 101
psychic development 7, 17
psychoanalysis 61, 91, 92, 94, 96

Qabalah 19, 21, 23, 25, 27, 29, 31, 34, 37-40, 42, 43, 45, 77, 95

Regardie, Israel 97
reincarnation 98, 99, 103, 104, 108
Richardson, Alan 108, 109
Ring-Pass-Not 52
Robert Boyle 50
Rosenrath, Knorr von 38

INDEX

Saving the Appearances 77
Scholem, Gershom 19, 37
Sea Priestess, The 94, 106, 107, 111
Secrets of Dr Taverner, The 92
Seed Atoms 106
self-help books 7
Sepher Yetzirah 25, 27
Shadow-of-a-Leaf 66-67
Shekinah 21, 22
Simeon ben Jochai 27
Society of the Inner Light 98, 99, 108
spiritual intention 11, 18
spiritual pathology 98, 106, 107
Steinbrecher, Edwin 102
Steiner, Rudolf 53, 70, 100
subconscious 15
superconscious 15

Tales of the Mermaid Tavern 65, 67
Tao of Physics, The 86
Tarot trumps 102-103
teaching schools 7-9, 60
Tennyson, Alfred 55, 56
Thomas Aquinas 35

thought-forms 110, 112
throne mysticism 24-25
Torch-Bearers, The 66
tracks in space 63
Treatise on Method 85
Tree of Life 12, 19-27, 30, 31, 37-45, 72, 73, 75, 80, 81, 95, 99
tsim-tsum 21

Veils of Negative Existence 21
Vision of Ezekiel 24
Vision of God Face to Face 23

War Letters of Dion Fortune 109
What Coleridge Thought 70, 100
Williams, Charles 58, 78, 111
Winged Bull, The 94
Wordsworth, William 17, 66, 69, 74
Wynn Westcott, Dr William 93

Yoga 15, 93

Zohar, The 27, 37, 38

Ingram Content Group UK Ltd.
Milton Keynes UK
UKHW040704200323
418846UK00001B/71